Developing Inclusive Mobile Apps

Building Accessible Apps for iOS and Android

Rob Whitaker

Apress®

Developing Inclusive Mobile Apps: Building Accessible Apps for iOS and Android

Rob Whitaker
Derby, UK

ISBN-13 (pbk): 978-1-4842-5813-2   ISBN-13 (electronic): 978-1-4842-5814-9
https://doi.org/10.1007/978-1-4842-5814-9

Managing Director, Apress Media LLC: Welmoed Spahr
Acquisitions Editor: Aaron Black
Development Editor: James Markham
Coordinating Editor: Jessica Vakili

Distributed to the book trade worldwide by Springer Science+Business Media New York, 233 Spring Street, 6th Floor, New York, NY 10013. Phone 1-800-SPRINGER, fax (201) 348-4505, e-mail orders-ny@springer-sbm.com, or visit www.springeronline.com. Apress Media, LLC is a California LLC and the sole member (owner) is Springer Science + Business Media Finance Inc (SSBM Finance Inc). SSBM Finance Inc is a **Delaware** corporation.

For information on translations, please e-mail rights@apress.com, or visit http://www.apress.com/rights-permissions.

Apress titles may be purchased in bulk for academic, corporate, or promotional use. eBook versions and licenses are also available for most titles. For more information, reference our Print and eBook Bulk Sales web page at http://www.apress.com/bulk-sales.

Any source code or other supplementary material referenced by the author in this book is available to readers on GitHub via the book's product page, located at www.apress.com/978-1-4842-5813-2.

For more detailed information, please visit http://www.apress.com/source-code.

Printed on acid-free paper

Table of Contents

About the Author

Rob Whitaker is an iOS development engineer currently working for Capital One in the United Kingdom, where he works on their credit card servicing app. At Capital One, one of his major projects has been working with the Royal National Institute of Blind People. The project has created a high level of accessibility for Capital One's mobile app through expert assessments and user testing.

Rob has been building iOS apps since the launch of the iOS SDK, as a hobbyist, independent developer, and a full-time engineer. Rob is most passionate about making great mobile experiences that work for everyone on both iOS and Android. He blogs on this subject at MobileA11y.com and @MobileA11y on Twitter. Here you can find discussion on techniques and tools for making accessible and inclusive mobile apps.

Rob has spoken at many conferences and meetups on the subject of accessibility and inclusion. This includes iOSDevUK, CodeMobile, and NSLondon in the United Kingdom. He's also spoken further afield in Washington, DC, and at the CSUN Assistive Technology Conference in Anaheim, California.

Rob lives in the middle of the United Kingdom where he enjoys views over a national park when the weather is bad. When the weather is good, he enjoys getting out into the national park with his wife and dog.

You can find him on Twitter @RobRWAPP.

About the Technical Reviewer

Ahmed Bakir is an iOS author, teacher, and entrepreneur. He has worked on over 30 mobile projects, ranging from advising startups to architecting apps for Fortune 500 companies. In 2014, he published his first book, *Beginning iOS Media App Development*, followed by the first edition of *Program the Internet of Things with Swift for IOS* in 2016 and its second edition in 2018. In 2015, he was invited to develop courses and teach iOS development at UCSD-Extension. He is currently building cool stuff in Tokyo! You can find him online at devatelier.com.

Acknowledgments

Such an enormous number of people have helped me in various ways with the content of this book. Listing each person would be a full chapter. It's safe to say if I've ever spoken to you in person or online about digital accessibility or inclusion, you've had an impact on this book for the better. This extends to the many great talks, blog posts, tweets, and more that I've consumed on the topic. Thank you all for spreading the word about mobile inclusion.

Thank you to Daniel Devesa, Jonathan Rothwell, Paul Hudson, Jon Gibbins, StuffMC, and a couple of anonymous sources – all of whom have furnished me with advice and fielded my questions that have shaped the book.

Thank you to Jessica Vakili, Aaron Black, Ahmed Bakir, James Markham, and all at Apress who have made the book possible. I hugely appreciate the work you have put in to make this project a reality. I'm also grateful to Matt Clark for the illustration he kindly provided.

A big thank you to all my colleagues at Capital One for humoring my constant accessibility talk. You are proof that it's possible to create a pro-accessibility culture among a large development team. I especially want to mention Weiran Zang, Kasey Smith, and Harriet Matthews for their encouragement and Matthew Flint who is responsible for forging me into a semi-competent engineer.

Finally, thanks to my family, especially my wife Claire for having infinite patience, understanding, and support. Thanks also to my dog Bella, to whom I have read most of this book and who was polite enough to not look bored for most of it.

CHAPTER 1

Accessibility

My interest in accessibility began back in 2010 while I was the manager of a small Apple reseller. A great privilege of working in technology retail is that you get to meet a vast range of people at different stages in their technology journey. Some customers ask original questions that take a great deal of research to find the right answer. Others have never touched anything you or I might call a "computer" before and are starting at the very beginning.

In June of 2010, Apple released the iPhone 4. After this, I began to notice the number of our customers coming into the store who used British Sign Language (BSL) as their first language was significantly increasing. From interactions with some of these customers, it became clear why this was: With the release of the iPhone 4, Apple had also released a brand-new feature – FaceTime.

FaceTime and other video calling features like it were an incredible improvement on usability for our customers using BSL. FaceTime makes up just one out of a raft of accessibility features that are part of modern smartphones, and landline telephones before that.

The Telephone and Accessible Innovation

One aim of inclusive technology is to create a comparable experience for all users, a topic we will revisit in Chapter 2. Alexander Graham Bell did not have the benefit of inclusive thinking to guide his invention. As a result,

© Rob Whitaker 2020
R. Whitaker, *Developing Inclusive Mobile Apps*,
https://doi.org/10.1007/978-1-4842-5814-9_1

the environment wasn't ready to facilitate him to design the telephone with accessibility at the forefront. In the following years, we'd have to work to add assistive technology. Many technologies have been added, such as the Telecommunications Device for the Deaf that we'll cover shortly. Short message service (or SMS), voice recognition systems, and video calls have all been accessible advances for the telephone. While these assistive technologies have made improvements for people with disabilities, the additions are not seamless. The phone has a long history associated with making the device more usable for people with specific needs. Today, mobile still leads with accessible innovation.

Most of us have been able to use the telephone, as intended, to speak to friends, family, businesses, in the next room, next country, or across the globe since its invention almost 150 years ago. Consider, if this isn't already the case, that your primary, or perhaps only, form of communication is sign language. This immediately renders the telephone useless. The phone is a ubiquitous invention, but it presents content in a single medium – audio. Innovation has helped those of us unable to hear to make the phone more accessible.

Telecommunications Device for the Deaf

The Telecommunications Device for the Deaf is often alternatively known as TDD, TTY, textphone, or minicom. It is a QUERTY keyboard and teleprinter display invented in the 1960s that connects to a landline telephone (Figure 1-1). With these additions, the TDD allows people with limited speech or hearing to type their conversation. Conversations can be direct to other TDD users or to an operator relaying the conversation to a non-TDD user.

Figure 1-1. *An example of a Telecommunications Device for the Deaf*

While the TDD is an essential tool for many people, it's not an equivalent to the phone. If you've ever used one of these services, you'll know the interaction is slower and more awkward compared to a standard phone call, in the same way it might be if you were having a conversation through an interpreter into a foreign spoken language. The TDD is accessible, but it isn't inclusive.

Video Calling

FaceTime today is a technology we all take for granted. Most of us involved in creating software will use some form of video call system almost daily – Skype, Google Hangouts, Zoom, or any number of alternative systems. But, a decade ago, to be able to see anyone, anywhere else in the world instantly in high-quality video, and to have a conversation with them was pretty groundbreaking. Yet for our deaf and hard of hearing customers, it was more than groundbreaking. It was transformational to their ability to communicate. The ability to sign conversations finally makes the telephone a comparable experience.

FaceTime didn't become an Apple product because Apple set out to make an excellent accessibility tool for sign language users. Apple set out to create a great product that would work for everyone. By ensuring that it works for everyone, and considering accessibility throughout the project, Apple is super-serving one specific audience.

Mobile Innovation

Mobile is packed full of accessibility features like FaceTime. Google Assistant and Siri Shortcuts reduce the requirement for accuracy. This helps people with learning difficulties. It also reduces the number of touches required helping with motor issues. Screen Time and Safari Reader help to minimize distractions – ideal for people with attention-deficit disorders or those with mental health problems who can find relief in focus. Dictation, spelling correction, predictive text, voice memos, vibration on alerts, third-party keyboards, and external keyboard support are all examples of assistive technologies. There's a good chance you use these daily, without ever considering them an accessibility feature.

Consider the Telecommunications Device for the Deaf we previously discussed. The inventors needed some method to allow digital text to pass over a wire. Their resulting invention was the MODEM. Without the MODEM, much of our modern digital society would simply not be possible. Next time you're at the corner of a street with a roller case or a buggy – the dropped curb, initially put in place to help wheelchair users, means you won't have to lift your heavy item to the street level. Great accessibility shouldn't be an obscure feature that only a small number of people use. At its best, accessibility should be a first-class citizen of the product or service you are creating and should benefit everyone.

Clearly then, accessibility is not just something that benefits those who have a disability. It has a much broader reach for customizability for all users. While disabled users may gain the most, every one of your users stands to benefit from the consideration you give accessibility. At its best, accessibility is inclusion for every one of your customers. We'll cover this more in Chapter 2. For now, let's get a little more context on what we mean by disability, especially disability in a digital context.

What Is Disability?

In January 2019, a photo was shared widely on social media (Figure 1-2). The photo featured an otherwise unremarkable woman going about her business walking along an inner-city street. This lady had two features that led to Facebook users commenting, however. This lady was using a smartphone, nothing unusual there, but this lady also had a white cane to assist her in navigating the city.

Figure 1-2. *A person using a cane and a smartphone. Posted to Facebook with the caption "If you can see what's wrong say I see it 😎"*

The white cane has been used since World War I as a tool to help blind and partially sighted people, many of whom use it to assist them navigating the built environment by feeling the street around them for obstacles and clues such as tactile paving. One of the cane's primary purposes, however, may not be immediately apparent to those of us who don't use it; the hint is in the color of the cane. White canes are, indeed, white. Because they are white, they are a clear indication to those of us who see it, that the person holding it may not see us. It's a clue for us as drivers to take extra caution and as pedestrians to ensure we allow the person room to pass.

Perhaps this was the case with the lady in the photo posted to Facebook. Maybe she had poor eyesight and was using the cane predominately as a hint to fellow pedestrians that she may not see them. Possibly she does use her cane to feel for the built environment around her as she can't see items at a distance but still has vision closer to her eyes and so can continue to use her phone.

I don't presume that anyone reading this book would, as many Facebook users did, question this lady's ability, or lack thereof, mainly because you likely work in mobile and know there is a raft of display accommodations she could be making to improve her experience and allow her to use her smartphone. Perhaps she has large text or zoom enabled. Maybe she is using inverted colors or increased contrast. Possibly she isn't even looking at the screen at all – she could be using a screen reader with the screen curtain enabled, and this is just the natural way to hold a phone while using it. It's impossible to understand someone else's experiences without asking them. If you want to really understand how someone uses your app, this is precisely what I'd recommend – ask them.

All this is to say – disability is not, much like anything in life, merely a binary state. It is not possible to divide the world up into two groups – those who are disabled and those who are able-bodied; or, in our precedent example, blind and sighted. There is a large section in between – from those of us who have to wear reading glasses for specific tasks through to those of us who experience no light perception at all, via cataracts, color blindness, and others. Visual impairments vary from person to person, over time, as do all disabilities. As I'm sure we're all aware, not all disabilities are visible.

So then, if disability is a broad spectrum, how do we define it? The best way to highlight what I think disability means is to use the World Health Organization's definitions. In 1980, WHO established disability in these terms:

> *In the context of health experience, a disability is any restriction or lack of ability (resulting from an impairment) to perform an activity in the manner or within the range considered normal for a human being.*[1]

—World Health Organization, 1980

In other words, they defined disability as a feature of that person, something that makes a disabled person different from the rest of us and unable to do the things we might reasonably expect a "normal" person to be able to. I think we can settle on disability being a "restriction or lack of ability." But a problem arises with the last part – "the range considered normal for a human being." The word "normal" here raises more questions than it answers – What is a normal human being? What would we expect this fictitious normal human being to do? Who decides what is normal? Should I be concerned if I don't match the considered definition of normal? The answer to all these questions is simple – there is no such thing. There is no "normal" for human beings. Without wishing to sound like a preschool kids TV show – we are all wonderfully different in our own ways.

---

[1]https://download.microsoft.com/download/b/0/d/b0d4bf87-09ce-4417-8f28-d60703d672ed/inclusive_toolkit_manual_final.pdf

Visit the WHO's web site today, and you'll see an updated definition:

> *Disability is not just a health problem. It is a complex phe-*
> *nomenon, reflecting the interaction between features of a per-*
> *son's body and features of the society in which he or she lives.*
> *Overcoming the difficulties faced by people with disabilities*
> *requires interventions to remove environmental and social*
> *barriers.*[2]

—World Health Organization

This definition considers disability not as a problem with people but a problem with the society we have built. This definition recognizes that everyone is different and has different abilities, knowledge, and skills, and that to be different is normal. Therefore, if someone struggles with an aspect of our society, this is not a problem with the person. Instead, it is a problem with the culture that has allowed this to happen. This definition also recognizes that disability is not about whether someone can use steps to enter a building. Instead, it is about the systems on which we build our society, such as the way we might make someone with learning difficulties feel if we make them complete a large form or how someone with mental health problems may feel trapped by a prescriptive system. This is known as the social model of disability.

Major Minority

People identifying as experiencing disability are a minority. But together they make up one of the largest minority groups across Europe and North America. In the United States, an estimated 27% of people have a disability, that's 85.3 million people.[3] This puts people with disabilities on par with most

---

[2]www.who.int/topics/disabilities/en/

[3]www.census.gov/content/dam/Census/library/publications/2018/demo/p70-
152.pdf

populous 3 states combined. In the United Kingdom, 22% of people report having a disability, nearly 14 million people.[4] Globally, over a billion people experience disability, approximately 15% of the global population.[5] There's a good chance your organization's device support policy covers devices with a far smaller market share than your total customers with disabilities.

Having read this far, I hope I have convinced you of the importance of considering your users with different abilities. As a result, the quality of accessibility in your personal work will, I'm sure, be much higher. The maximum impact for customers with disabilities, however, will happen because your business and your colleagues share your conviction for making great accessible experiences. In the next sections, we'll cover ways you can do this.

The Business Case for Accessibility

Ultimately, the case for accessibility is simple – that it is the right thing to do to. Prejudicing your customers because of their abilities is wrong. But, I realize that if you're a manager, or you are making a case for an increased focus on accessibility to a business manager, then there are other considerations you need to include.

The US National Organization on Disability estimates that discretionary spend for people with disabilities is over US$200 billion.[6] In the United Kingdom, the spending power of disabled people and their families is referred to as the "Purple Pound." The Purple Pound is recognized as a crucial spending block for businesses. Evidence shows

---

[4] www.gov.uk/government/collections/family-resources-survey--2
[5] www.who.int/disabilities/infographic/en/
[6] www.dol.gov/odep/pubs/fact/diverse.htm

that companies which aren't considering digital accessibility lose out by causing disabled people to choose alternative services.[7] In the United Kingdom, the Purple Pound is worth an estimated £265 billion or US$336 billion.[8]

If an extra $200 billion in market value is not carrot enough for your business, there is a sizable legal stick too, one that can result in hefty fines and long-lasting reputational damage.

Accessibility Law

As with any law, national variations on accessibility law are vast.[9] Many countries have no laws governing accessibility at all. Where laws do exist, these will often concern the government or public sector only. Sometimes these will be pre-digital laws crudely adjusted through convention to fit digital channels. Many regulations are not explicitly focusing on digital accessibility; instead, they are more general nondiscrimination laws. You should seek legal advice to determine which rules apply to the markets you're operating in and how.

In this section, I cover two of the principal regions with digital accessibility laws with which the majority of us creating mobile apps will have to comply. This section is intended as a high-level overview and not as legal advice, so if you think these laws may apply to your business, I'd advise seeking out a professional opinion.

---

[7] http://clickawaypound.com/cap16finalreport.html

[8] www.barclayscorporate.com/client-experience/client-benefits/ supporting-economic-growth/

[9] www.w3.org/WAI/policies/

The United States

The United States has one of the world's oldest accessibility laws. Introduced in 1990, the Americans with Disabilities Act, known as the ADA.[10]

The ADA covers the government's requirements for ensuring accessibility from suppliers and within government-supplied services, such as schools. Included in the private sector are physical "places of public accommodations" – restaurants, theaters, and shops to you and me. The ADA is not explicit about digital content. But the department of justice who upholds the ADA maintains that the ADA is broad enough to govern digital experiences too. In a 2019 landmark case, Domino's Pizza chose to challenge this assertion. Taking the case to the Supreme Court, Domino's argued that the ADA didn't apply to their pizza ordering app. The Supreme Court ruled against Domino's. This sets a precedent that means the legal requirements for mobile accessibility are not a gray area. Other household names like the National Basketball Association, Netflix, and Beyoncé have all fallen foul of DOJ court rulings on the ADA.

Europe

The European Accessibility Act,[11] written in 2018, is a far more modern piece of legislation. The EAA uses as its reference accessibility legislation from across Europe. It also draws cues from the US ADA. The aim is to standardize the accessibility requirements for digital accessibility throughout Europe.

The EAA does not expressly establish accessibility standards for mobile or digital services as a whole. It does insist on the mobile accessibility standards for defined categories. These include E-commerce, banking,

---

[10]www.ada.gov

[11]https://eur-lex.europa.eu/legal-content/EN/TXT/?uri=COM:2015:0615:FIN

software services related to passenger transport, and software as part of a smartphone or smartphone operating system.

Requirements vary depending on your app's business category. In summary, some shared requirements include

- Provide for flexible magnification, contrast, and color.

- Provide alternatives to fine motor control.

- Provide information in more than one sensory channel. Or provide information in a format that the device can present in an alternative sensory channel.

- Provide alternatives for non-text content.

- Provide consistent interoperability with assistive technologies.

Advocating for Accessibility

One of the best ways to increase accessibility in your apps is to advocate for accessibility within your organization. When UX send you new designs, product asks for a new feature, or your team are refining stories, all of these are great times to advocate.

Don't criticize others' work. From my experience, colleagues do care about accessibility and want to do better. Sometimes they lack the knowledge and expertise to do this. Champion work when you can see accessibility has been considered, and congratulate when you know something will work well for users with different needs. Make small suggestions that will add up to an improved experience. Over time, you'll find your team will take this on board and will begin to think from an accessibility-first approach.

If your organization has multiple customer-facing software teams, you could consider starting an accessibility advocates network. Encourage someone from each group to get involved. Include UX, product, and maybe management too. Share knowledge and questions over a Slack channel. In some cases, it may be possible to find a budget for training, providing insight that you can cascade down to your teams. Consider running training sessions for other colleagues from what you have learned. Sharing some of the activities covered in the next section make for a great icebreaker.

Demonstrating Accessibility

One effective way to convince colleagues and managers that accessibility matters, and to make it clear why it matters to your customers, is to simulate some of the conditions that your customers may be experiencing. This way, colleagues can experience firsthand what it might be like to experience your app with different abilities. Be careful with these exercises, though. The purpose is to give some insight into your customer's experiences. People's takeaways from these exercises can sometimes be pity and fear of the disability.

I've included some exercises I've collected that provide rough approximations of certain (dis)abilities. For each of these activities, pick a different everyday smartphone task. Or, to make it more relevant to your organization, select a widely used flow from your app. Be aware that you may already be more familiar with your app because you made it. Make the task different each time to avoid getting too familiar with the flow.

SIMULATING BLINDNESS

iOS has an accessibility feature to use along with its inbuilt screen reader, VoiceOver, that allows users of the reader to maintain privacy. Called Screen Curtain, this feature turns off the image on the display, while keeping the touch screen active. As screen reader users already have the content of their personal device read aloud, this prevents them from unwittingly sharing personal content visually. A low-vision or blind user may not be aware private content is even visible, so keeping the screen on has little or no benefit. Plus, disabling it increases privacy and battery life. Screen Curtain gives us an excellent opportunity to get an idea of what it would be like to use a smartphone without visual feedback.

For this activity, pick an everyday task you might do with your phone. Adding a calendar event is a good option, or to make it more relevant to your organization, you could choose a typical flow from your app. Enable VoiceOver – read the section "Navigating with VoiceOver" in Chapter 6 before doing this. Then enable the Screen Curtain by triple tapping the screen with three fingers.

Now use the screen reader to navigate the phone and complete the task, without ever seeing what is on the screen. While those who use screen readers daily are likely to be more skilled at its use than the average engineering team, this should give you some insight into what aspects of smartphone use are harder when voice is the only feedback. If you are doing this as a group exercise, it will also give you an idea of how noisy environments can make screen reader use frustrating. It's the screen reader user's equivalent to someone waving their hand above your screen.

Stock Android doesn't have an equivalent feature. But some Samsung devices feature a setting called Dark Screen which has the same effect with TalkBack enabled.

SIMULATING ATTENTION DISORDERS

For this task, you'll need some small balloons or soft balls. Pick a job you'll do every day on a smartphone or a standard flow from your app. Your task is to complete this flow while keeping the balloon or ball in the air. While the analogy may be a little stretched, this should give you some insight into how easy it may be to use your app for customers with attention-deficit disorders, or perhaps as a parent of small children.

SIMULATING VISUAL IMPAIRMENTS

The Royal National Institute of Blind People from the United Kingdom has produced an app called EYEWARE. It's available for free from Apple's App Store[12] or the Google Play Store.[13] EYEWARE works best with Google Cardboard but does work without if you don't have them to hand.

The RNIB developed EYEWARE along with people with visual impairments to simulate what it's like to experience the world with a visual impairment. The app allows you to pick from several different kinds of impairment – from color blindness to cataracts, glaucoma, and more, including variations of each. Try out the settings, and complete your chosen task or tasks with different levels of vision. Consider how the use of color changes with color blindness, and how larger text is essential with cataracts, for example.

---

[12]https://apps.apple.com/us/app/eyeware/id1169994271
[13]https://play.google.com/store/apps/details?id=com. transportsystemscatapult.EyeWarePro&hl=en_US

Summary

- Sometimes, we make technology that excludes people with specific abilities. We can improve these by adding accessibility features. But these add-ons often feel like add-ons; they're not seamless.

- In the next chapter, we'll discuss digital inclusion. This is the ultimate aim of accessibility – to make technology that feels at home to everyone.

- Disability is not a binary state. We all have abilities and limits to those abilities. Disability happens when we have built something that doesn't work for someone with particular skills.

- There is a big business case for considering people's different abilities when building your app, a $200 billion business case. And that's just in the United States. Your business will also be bound by international accessibility legislation. If you aren't following these laws, you stand to receive a hefty fine and reputational damage.

We'll continue to look at the background of accessible technology in the next chapter. But we'll move away from considering accessibility as an extra. Instead, we'll consider inclusion and how we can make all of our users feel part of our app.

CHAPTER 2

Digital Inclusion

In this chapter, you'll discover a little about the history of inclusive thinking and what this means. We'll cover the fundamental tenets that hold up this thinking, and discuss the things that you should consider when creating software, such as the importance of remembering that your users are real people. We'll cover the single most critical skill any software engineer can have that comes hand in hand with taking pride in your work.

The History of Inclusive Thinking

Digital inclusion has its roots in architecture and product design. In the process of creating mobile apps, good design is essential. But a significant part still of the accessible experience of an app is created by those of us who aren't designers. Digital inclusion recognizes that everyone, including but not limited to designers, has a role to play in encouraging more accessible interactions.

Even if you're not a designer, I think it's worth our time covering some of the background of this school of design. This way, we can understand some of the mistakes that were made and steps taken to fix them. Plus, if you're an engineer, your job is to make designs a reality. So knowledge of the work that has influenced those designs will help you realize them.

© Rob Whitaker 2020
R. Whitaker, *Developing Inclusive Mobile Apps*,
https://doi.org/10.1007/978-1-4842-5814-9_2

Universal Design

Digital inclusion has its roots in universal design, a movement that began in the late 1960s and led to many commonplace accessibility improvements we see around us today. Architect and designer Ronald Mace coined the phrase universal design. He used it to describe the concept of designing usable products and the built environment for the most people possible, while crucially remaining aesthetically pleasing.

Fellow architect Selwyn Goldsmith, himself a wheelchair user, progressed the concept of universal design by championing the now ubiquitous dropped curb or curb cut (Figure 2-1). The curb cut allows wheelchair users or those with mobility issues to be able to cross the street more comfortably than with a standard raised curb. The dropped curb is also a prime example of how universal design helps as many people as possible. While initially intended to improve mobility for wheelchair users, it also allows parents with pushchairs and travelers with rolling cases.

Figure 2-1. *A curb cut providing step-free access to the street*

Universal design is a series of principles used by architects and product and industrial designers to guide them in achieving Ronald Mace's original aims. In 1997, North Carolina State University gathered some of the leading advocates of universal design, including Ronald Mace himself. Together they defined the seven principles of universal design.[1] These are

- Equitable use

- Flexibility in use

- Simple and intuitive use

- Perceptible information

- Tolerance for error

- Low physical effort

- Size and space for approach and use

I have summarized very briefly what each of these principles cover here. I've also given a quick outline of how each principle might apply to mobile. Some of the concepts here might be new, but we'll cover all of them in later chapters.

Equitable Use

Make the design appealing to all users. The design should be useful and marketable to people with diverse abilities. Avoid segregating or stigmatizing any users. Provide an identical experience for all users wherever possible. If you have to provide an alternative experience, make this equivalent. Consider privacy, security, and safety for all of your customers.

---

[1]https://projects.ncsu.edu/ncsu/design/cud/about_ud/udprinciplestext.htm

In a mobile setting, this might mean avoiding using colors that don't pass the WCAG 2.1 (Chapter 3) contrast ratio guidelines of 4.5:1.[2] Also, ensure your app works seamlessly with assistive technologies such as TalkBack and VoiceOver (Figure 2-2).

Figure 2-2. *VoiceOver navigating iOS' Weather app*

---

[2]"W3C Web Content Accessibility Guidelines (WCAG) 2.1", W3C, Accessed October 5, 2019. https://www.w3.org/TR/WCAG21/

Flexibility in Use

Your design accommodates a wide range of individual preferences and abilities. Provide choice, facilitate the user, and adapt to them.

Examples of this in mobile would include supporting varying text sizes. Allow multiple methods of input for text such as on-screen keyboard, dictation (Figure 2-3), or external keyboard. Both platforms offer your customer various customization settings; respect these as much as you can.

Figure 2-3. *Google's on screen keyboard allowing typing through dictation*

Simple and Intuitive

Ensure your design is easy to understand, regardless of the user's experience, knowledge, language skills, or current concentration level. Eliminate unnecessary complexity. Be consistent with user expectations and intuition. Accommodate a wide range of literacy and language skills. Arrange information in a manner that is consistent with its importance keeping the most critical information prominent. Provide effective prompting and feedback during and after task completion.

Stick to a standard design language throughout your app, including sticking with system-provided controls and conventions wherever possible. Summarize information carefully, but allow customers to drill down for detail if they would like more information. Keep the language simple and understandable. When your app requires user input, you should be explicit about what information you need and where. If your customer makes an error, make this clear and allow them to change it quickly.

Perceptible Information

Your design should communicate necessary information effectively to your user, regardless of ambient conditions or the user's sensory abilities. Use different modes (pictorial, verbal, tactile) for redundant presentation of essential information. Provide adequate contrast between foreground and background – we cover this more in Chapter 3. Provide compatibility with a variety of techniques or devices used by people with sensory limitations.

To meet this principle in mobile, we must ensure all content is accessible to the device's screen reader or any other assistive technology available on the device. Chapter 4 on the Android accessibility model and Chapter 6 on the iOS accessibility model will give you the tools to do this. Present your content in multiple means. Use a combination of color, shape, images text, and layout together to make your content meaningful (Figure 2-4). Your customer's screen reader will turn text content into audio content, but it can't do the same with text you provide as an image. For valuable content, consider offering this in an alternative means, such as a video.

Figure 2-4. *Android combining color, shape, text, and an image to convey meaning*

Tolerance for Error

Minimize the hazards and the adverse consequences of accidental or unintended actions. Arrange elements to minimize risks and errors: Make commonly used controls prominent. Provide warnings of dangers and mistakes. Advise your customer in advance if they are making a destructive change and allow them to back out. If your customer makes an error, highlight this clearly in position and allow them to change it effortlessly. Before committing to any action, let your customer review their response, and allow them to change or revert. Provide safety features so destructive effects can't happen by accident.

In mobile apps, this includes using clear and concise information on the consequences of each action when you ask your user to make a decision. Add friction to harmful or destructive actions and provide feedback to your customer on what to expect when they make the decision.

Low Physical Effort

Ensure customers can use your design efficiently and comfortably and with a minimum of fatigue. Minimize repetitive actions and sustained effort.

All the buttons on your interface should be within easy reach (Figure 2-5), especially on large-screen devices. Provide shortcuts to common areas of your app, and support Google Assistant or Siri Shortcuts where possible.

Figure 2-5. *Shortcuts for common features within easy reach at the bottom of the screen*

Size and Space for Approach and Use

The final principle is mostly appropriate for physical items. The principle states you should provide proper size and space for approach, reach, manipulation, and use regardless of user's body size, posture, or mobility. Make reach to all components comfortable, and accommodate variations in hand and grip size.

We can meet this guideline by making our interfaces adaptable to different screen sizes and text sizes. Ensure your app works with Switch Control and Switch Access, as well as allowing keyboard navigation; also, Voice Control and Voice Access (Figure 2-6), allowing your customers to control your app with virtually no movement whatsoever. Any interactive elements should be at least 44px square so as not to insist on fine motor control.

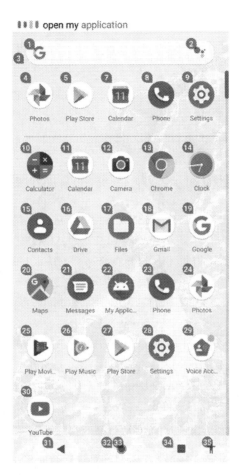

Figure 2-6. *Android's Voice Access feature allowing navigation without touching the screen*

These universal design principles have led to the creation of many items we would consider to be every day. We may not think of many of these products as "accessibility" features. Consider audiobooks, automatic doors, high-contrast signage, and flexible drinking straws. All of these products were created following universal design guidelines. They serve many people with different abilities but are improvements for everyone else as well. This is what we should be striving for in our apps. Our ideal aim is to create an experience that includes everyone.

Universal design considers disability and considers what you can achieve in modifying the design to help people experiencing that disability, thereby reducing the barriers for the use of the product. Reducing barriers widens the market for potential users. However, as universal design was developed in an era before digital, the approach has been tailored to physical products.

Inclusive Design

Inclusive design extends on the gains made by universal design. It is generally more tailored to digital interactions. While universal design considers disability, inclusive design considers individuals and tends towards a more accessible-first approach. Inclusive design takes a big step forward in recognizing that disability is not a permanent, binary state but a spectrum. Inequalities in people's abilities are typical and vary as a function of time or situation. Inclusive design does this by considering people's needs as permanent, temporary, situational, or changing. By improving an experience for people with specific needs and considering these needs in the first instance, we can extend this benefit to work for a broader population, therefore improving the experience for everyone at some point in their life.

Digital accessibility consultants The Paciello Group[3] helped define the seven principals of inclusive design. They set up *inclusivedesignprinciples.org*[4] to document them. These principles are

- Provide comparable experience

- Consider situation

---

[3] www.paciellogroup.com

[4] "Inclusive Design Principles", Inclusive Design Principles, Accessed October 5, 2019. https://inclusivedesignprinciples.org.

- Be consistent

- Give control

- Offer choice

- Prioritize content

- Add value

I have outlined the principles and how they apply to mobile in the following.

Provide Comparable Experience

Ensure your interface provides a comparable experience for all. Allow people to accomplish tasks in a way that suits their needs without undermining the quality of the content. You can provide audio descriptions or a transcript of a video in your app. These would make your original content accessible. But does this alternative capture the essence and tone of the original? Mobile interactions have an exceptional quality to surprise and delight their users. You should make sure all of your users get such a rich experience, even if they are using an assistive technology.

An example provided by inclusivedesignprinciples.org is that of Android live regions (Figure 2-7). Live regions are an area of the screen that automatically reports to assistive technologies when the content changes. TalkBack will read this content without the user having to navigate focus to this content. iOS doesn't have a live region feature, but you can create the same yourself using accessibility notifications. We cover these in Chapter 8.

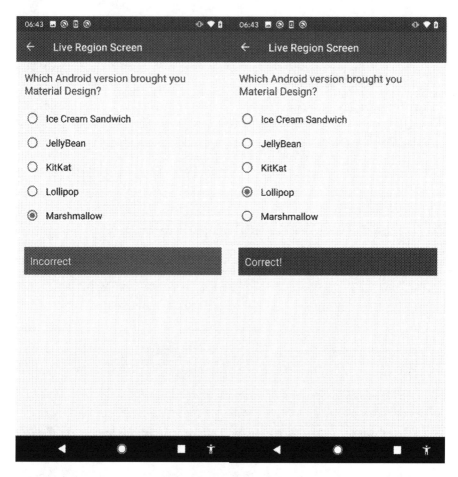

Figure 2-7.   *The "correct!"/"incorrect" area of the screen is a live region. TalkBack will automatically announce this content when it changes, without the user losing focus*

Consider Situation

People use your interface in different situations. Make sure your interface delivers a valuable experience to people regardless of their circumstances.

Consider using your phone in bright sunlight, audio, and haptic feedback along with high-contrast colors which will help in this situation. Providing subtitles or closed captions (Figure 2-8) on your video content allows parents to watch videos with the sound down without disturbing their sleeping children.

So, welcome to WWDC.

Figure 2-8. *Captions for videos allow people to watch video without disturbing others, as well as helping people with hearing impairments*

Be Consistent

Use familiar conventions, and apply them consistently to promote familiarity and understanding. This consistency applies both within your app and against the system you're running on.

Don't reinvent the wheel in your design. When you're building the design stand on the shoulders of giants by using the controls that Android and iOS provide for you, feel free to subclass the controls to add a feature or appearance you need, but starting with these as a base will give you so much extra for free. Your user will feel at home because their interactions will feel familiar, and Apple and Google already have you covered for many accessibility features.

Give Control

Ensure that people are in control. Your customers should be able to access and interact with content in their preferred way. Do not suppress or disable the ability to change standard platform settings such as orientation or font size (Figure 2-9). Additionally, avoid content changes that have not been initiated by your user unless there is a way to control it.

There are ways as a developer to disable some assistive features. For example, you can create an app that doesn't support scaling text sizes. This might mean you get a pixel-perfect design, but it will significantly affect your user's ability to use your app comfortably.

Figure 2-9. *iOS dynamic test styles at their smallest and largest settings. Supporting these is important for your customer and requires a flexible design*

Offer Choice

Consider providing different ways for people to complete tasks, especially tasks that are complex or nonstandard. There is often more than one way to complete a task. You cannot assume what someone's preferred method might be. By providing alternatives for layout and task completion, you offer people choices that suit them and their circumstances at the time.

A great example of this is deleting an email in iOS' Mail app. I can do this with a tap (Figure 2-10), a swipe (Figure 2-12), or a long press (Figure 2-11). This lets me, as a user, pick the option that is fastest for how I use the app.

Figure 2-10. *Deleting mail with a tap*

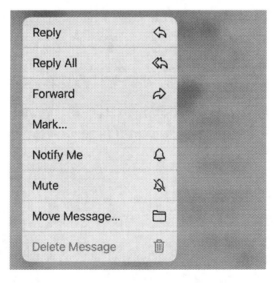

Figure 2-11. *Deleting mail with a long press*

Figure 2-12. *Deleting mail with a swipe*

Prioritize Content

Help users focus on core tasks, features, and information by prioritizing them within the content and layout. Identify the core purpose of the interface and then the content and features needed to fulfil that purpose. Interfaces can be challenging to understand when core features are not clearly exposed and prioritized.

Structure your content logically and mark headings with a heading trait or role. When you launch an email app, you're not presented with a list of mailboxes and folders to pick from. You're shown an inbox because this is the most essential feature. Standard features should be simple and always available. More complex actions should be possible but not prominent. Making everything available at once makes for a confusing interface. Consider placing advanced controls behind a secondary gesture such as a long press.

Add Value

Consider the value of features and how they improve the experience for different users. Consider device features such as voice, geolocation, camera, and vibration APIs and how integration with connected devices or a second screen could provide choice.

This is the area of inclusive design where mobile stands head and shoulders above other platforms. Mobile devices are full of sensors and feedback modes. External devices such as smart home, screens, or external controllers can be connected wirelessly. Picker controls on both platforms use haptics to provide tactile feedback to users when something has changed (Figure 2-13). While also being a satisfying experience, this is an essential feedback mode for customers with visual impairments, helping them determine when they have made a change.

Figure 2-13. *Setting an alarm on Android. Haptic feedback is provided when moving between minute/ hour intervals*

Persona Spectrum

One of the greatest proponents of inclusive design in software is Microsoft.[5] Microsoft has introduced a tool they call the Persona Spectrum (Figure 2-14).[6] The Persona Spectrum helps us to consider what inclusive design means to the people who use our software.

Consider, as inclusive design does, that we class disability as permanent, temporary, or situational. An example of a permanent disability may be the loss of an upper extremity. Losing an arm would make many everyday interactions difficult, and some may be even impossible. For this person, improving your app might mean ensuring all your buttons are within easy reach of the thumb of the hand that is holding the phone. Or even better, add voice control features. In doing this, you would also help to make your app more usable for people who have recently experienced an arm injury and are using a sling. Arm injuries are a temporary impairment – we would hope at least. Our customer with a broken arm will regain full use of their limb in a month or so. With this improvement, you would also be helping new parents. New parents may spend much of their time with the use of one hand, while they use the other to hold or feed their infant, control a pushchair, or hold a hand. In this example, our new parent has a situational impairment. The use of their second limb is restored once their child falls asleep or is handed to another family member.

---

[5]Access more on their Inclusive Design program at `www.microsoft.com/design/inclusive/`.

[6]"Inclusive", Microsoft Design, 2016. `https://download.microsoft.com/download/b/0/d/b0d4bf87-09ce-4417-8f28-d60703d672ed/inclusive_toolkit_manual_final.pdf`.

For this example, Microsoft did some research to highlight how thinking this way can have a great benefit to your customers:

> *In the United States, 26,000 people a year suffer from loss of upper extremities. But when we include people with temporary and situational impairments, the number is greater than 20M.*
>
> —Microsoft Inclusive Design Toolkit Manual[7]

---

[7]"Inclusive," Microsoft Design, Citing research from The United States Census Bureau, Limbs for Life Foundation, Amputee Coalition, MedicineHealth.com, CDC.gov, Disability Statistics Center at the UCSF.

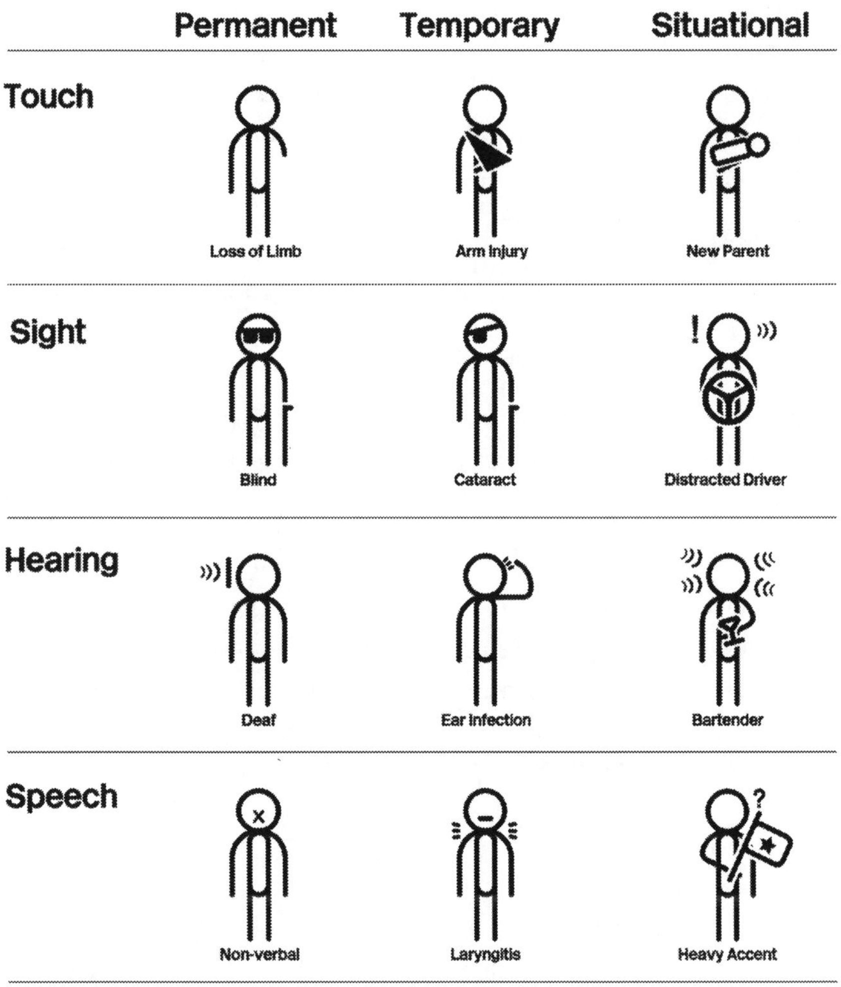

	Permanent	Temporary	Situational
Touch	Loss of Limb	Arm Injury	New Parent
Sight	Blind	Cataract	Distracted Driver
Hearing	Deaf	Ear Infection	Bartender
Speech	Non-verbal	Laryngitis	Heavy Accent

Figure 2-14. *Examples of Persona Spectra*

These examples provided by Microsoft also show examples of visual, auditory, and verbal persona spectra. A blind user would appreciate you considering how they would use your app without vision. This would also benefit someone who had recently had an eye operation, or someone who is currently driving and can't look at their device's screen.

Considering how your app functions for deaf people will help people with an ear infection or people who work in a noisy environment. A person who uses nonverbal communication would benefit from the same considerations as would help a temporary condition like laryngitis, or a situation like communicating with someone with a heavy accent.

NEW SPECTRUMS

Can your team create new examples of the Persona Spectrum?

Consider one of your customers with a permanent disability. What temporary or situational scenarios you would solve for if you improve your app for those people?

Consider the situation of a customer being in the wilderness. What features can you add that would help this user? How would that help people with temporary or permanent impairments? What about a customer who suffers from anxiety? What improvements can you make to give this customer a better experience, and how will that benefit others?

Digital Inclusion

Making software in an agile organization consists of more than implementing a screen as a designer has prescribed. There is much we can take from the design approach to inclusion. But not all of it is relevant to those of us who aren't designers, and much doesn't directly apply to the modern digital world.

We need a digital-first approach to inclusion, one that constitutes for a more rounded, high-level set of convictions. A strategy that recognizes everyone within the organization has a role to play in ensuring the service created is suitable for the highest number of people possible. Developers, with their advanced platform knowledge, constitute a significant part of this process. An essential part of digital inclusion is realizing that people with disabilities, while important, are not the only minority who want to use our service. Other factors such as age, gender, education, social grouping, income, and sexual orientation can all have an effect on how we experience technology. I have summarized my suggestions on what would make up the principles of digital inclusion in the following.

Empathetic

Considering others and recognizing that everyone is an individual with different in knowledge, experience, and ability and acknowledging that this makes people's experience of your app different – arguably, this is the most key tenet of digital inclusion, and we will cover this in its own section.

Situational

Not all barriers to using your app or service come from people's physical abilities. Inclusion means considering people's situation as a whole. This includes their skills but also other factors: financial, gender, digital literacy, mental health, and first language, among others. Realize that all these factors affect how someone may use your app.

Institutional

The software your organization creates mirrors your organization itself. Consider how the almost libertarian viewpoints of some social media leaders have led to platforms where almost anything goes, including at times racism, election interference, and harassment. Everyone in an organization can play a role in improving the accessibility of an app for the app's users and arguably has a responsibility to do this. In the following section, we take a look at what we mean by users and who these people are.

Users

In software engineering, we usually create products for our "users." It's sometimes said, in a quote often attributed to data visualization pioneer Edward Tufte, that calling people "users" is a habit we exclusively share with drug dealers. Except that's probably not true either. Drug dealers, I would imagine, still call their customers "customers" because that's what they are. It's really only the police and the media who employ the word "users." I don't intend to police the language you use, but let's take a look at why we should have a second thought about using that word.

Individuals

I don't believe there is anything inherently wrong in using the word users; in fact, I do use the term throughout this book. The problem is that this word can often hide who we're really making software for – *individuals*. Each and every one of your users is an individual, each one with their own individual wants, needs, abilities, experiences, and requirements for your software.

Employing the word "users" can result in falling into the trap of thinking of users as one group – an amalgamation of people who are out there somewhere in the world using your app, a group of people that you'll never meet and never know. This form of "group think" leads to creating a "one-size-fits-all" solution that, like everything claiming to be "one size fits all," in reality fits no one.

The great thing about you is that no one else is you. No one else has your skills and experiences. In the same way, you have never met a "normal" person, because nobody is normal. Everybody sees and experiences the world differently because they have seen and done things differently. Remember that time you had a bizarre bug in your app that happened because one person was using your app in a way you could have never envisaged? We've all had that experience. People do unpredictable things precisely because they think and act differently. What may have been an inconceivable combination of actions to you may seem entirely reasonable to someone using your app. Conversely, things which may appear obvious to you are going to be incomprehensible to some of the people using your app.

It is entirely natural when creating anything to be consumed by others to build it for people based on our own experiences. The problem with doing this is that you, or any of the other people in your office, won't be the main consumers of the product you are creating. While everyone is different, everyone working in a tech company office is, most likely, less different in some crucial ways than almost everyone else. There's a good chance if you're working in tech that you know tech pretty well and you've probably used quite a lot of it. Maybe you even enjoy using it; this is not the experience of a good many people.

Vasilis van Gemert, lecturer in applied science, warns us of the danger of thinking we are our own users.

> *In the past 25 years we have been designing [software] mostly for people who design [software].*
>
> —Vasilis van Gemert[8]

Your Experiences

Think about your group of friends and your colleagues, and think about your family. All of these groups you, hopefully, get on with, but there are subtle differences.

---

[8]van Gemert, Vasilis. "Exclusive Design", Exclusive Design, Accessed October 8, 2019. `https://exclusive-design.vasilis.nl/`.

Your friends are likely to be similar to you because you've chosen to hang out with them, and because they're your friends, I can already tell they're going to be awesome. Perhaps they don't work in tech, but there's a good chance that because you do, they will have a pretty high level of digital literacy. They will usually be a similar age to you, come from a similar background, and crucially enjoy many of the same things you do.

Your work colleagues are likely to be more varied, but there will still be things you have in common that are not representative of most people. You're all of working age and able to work. You all earn a similar amount of money (comparable to the general population). And you'll all have experience and interest in the industry in which you're working. Compare this to your family. Most of us will be able to think of at least one family member who doesn't use the Internet, maybe a family member who has a disability or for whom English is not their first language. Your family will make up a much more varied group than your friends and probably even your colleagues.

Considering these three groups and how they are different is probably the best example you can take from your personal experiences. But thinking about all these people combined will give you just a few hundred, at most, examples of how people's lives govern their knowledge of technology. The world is made up of almost 8 billion people.[9] So to get a representative survey of people's experiences of technology, you need 1000 examples as a minimum. And your sampling method of only choosing people connected to you in some way would not pass scrutiny.

> *If we use our own abilities as a baseline, we make things that are easy for some people to use, but difficult for everyone else.*
>
> —Microsoft Design[10]

---

[9]"Current World Population", Worldometer, Accessed October 13, 2019.
 http://www.worldometers.info/world-population/.
[10]"Inclusive," Microsoft Design.

The best way to fix this is to speak to real people. We discuss user testing in Chapter 11. Hopefully, your organization will already be doing some form of user testing. Don't write this off as an activity for design or product. Engineering can learn a lot too.

YOUR NETWORK

Here's a quick exercise to highlight why considering people you know is likely not representative of your customers. Make a list of the top five people you trust. These can be colleagues, friends, or family – people who you would go to for advice. Do this before reading on. Now add yourself to the list.

Now, list some of their traits. Use the same characteristics for each person. How old are they? What is their gender? List their race, sexual orientation, employment status, religion, and first language. Make a note of any disability you're aware of. There are probably other examples of traits you can think of. It's ok here to be honest and keep your answers private.

Take a look at your answers for each. My guess for most people is that these traits will look closely aligned. That's ok. The purpose of this exercise is not to shame you into expanding your network, simply to highlight that the people who are close to you are likely closer to you than you may have thought.

PEOPLE PROFILES

A great technique to help your whole team consider your customers as individuals is to create profiles. Have some fun creating a backstory. Consider what the person wants to do with your app and why. Think of the person's circumstances, experiences, and abilities. Most importantly, give your person a name, and refer to them by that name. Use Table 2-1 to guide you in creating a persona.

Table 2-1. *Profile sections*

Person name	Have fun choosing a name, but it's essential to refer to this person by name once you've created the profile
Age	Give an approximate age range
Gender	Remember that approximately 2% of the US population doesn't identify as either male or female[11]
Immediate family	Do they have dependents, either children or adults they care for? Are they married, live with family, or perhaps live alone?
Job and income	Your person could be employed, unemployed, self-employed, underemployed, or hugely successful in their career. Perhaps they are a lottery winner
Disability	Around 14% of people globally experience disability.[12] You should aim for a range of profiles that reflect different disabilities and none at all
Backstory	Go wild. Or not. Remember this profile is intended to represent a real person, but feel free to have some fun here
Why does this person want to use your app?	What will your app do for them? Is this a choice, or do they have to use your app for some reason?

---

[11]Cummings, William. "When asked their sex, some are going with option 'X'", USA Today, June 27, 2017. https://eu.usatoday.com/story/news/2017/06/21/third-gender-option-non-binary/359260001/.

[12]"Better health for people with disabilities: infographic", World Health Organization, Accessed October 12, 2019. www.who.int/disabilities/infographic/en/.

Empathy

Software is not made up of cold, unthinking algorithms. Sometimes this is used as a weak defense for bad decisions made in software's name. More importantly, it plays down your skills as a developer. It hides the reality that creating software is a craft and that those of us who make it are craftspeople in the most real sense of the word. We build beautiful software by hand and genuinely care about what goes into it as much as the end result. We're always sharpening our skills and expanding our personal toolbox.

I want to propose that one of the greatest, and most overlooked, tools a software craftsperson can have is empathy – the ability to understand that many other people, unlike you, will be directly affected by the decisions you make when creating an app. This has to be the central tenet of digital inclusion. Empathy is not a skill you can learn by having the highest number of commits to a project or having the most stars on GitHub. It is a tool you can only improve by taking a genuine interest in people and your craft.

Many books will tell you the essential skills required to be a great engineer; this is not the intended purpose of this book. There is one list I discovered that I feel are necessary skills for being a real software craftsperson:

- Openness toward feelings and esthetics

- Dealing with people

- Cooperative

- Work–life balance[13]

---

[13]Konger, Kaite, "Exclusive: Here's The Full 10-Page Anti-Diversity Screed Circulating Internally at Google [Updated]", Gizmodo. May 8, 2017. `https://gizmodo.com/exclusive-heres-the-full-10-page-anti-diversity-screed-1797564320`

The author of this list, however, never intended them as a guide for being a better engineer. Instead, precisely the opposite. These are all examples given by alt-right former Google employee James Damore in his notorious "Google memo." This list was intended as criticism on female software engineers. Essential reading on gender subjects[14] would tell you these examples are based on outdated, discredited research.

Conversely, they serve as a fantastic set of desirable skills for anyone working in software. By ensuring our teams have the highest possible range of life experience, we can use this experience to help inform our decisions. If you have a male-only team, you're excluding the experiences of 50% of people.

I mention Damore because his false assertions on diversity are in many ways the antithesis to this book. In a section entitled "De-emphasize Empathy," Damore states that empathy causes us to "favor individuals similar to us, and harbor other irrational and dangerous biases." What I would like you to take away from this book is the exact opposite of what Damore is saying. We should emphasize empathy precisely because it helps us to recognize and overcome our subconscious bias toward those who are similar to us. It is only possible to do empathy with emotion and a deep personal understanding of what is right. With the expanded sphere of experience that empathetic feeling gives us, we can then unemotionally reason to overcome these challenges.

Empathy As a Motivation

So, you're empathetic. You want to make a difference. You want to fix things for people with disabilities. This is a noble aim, but is it helping people with disabilities, or is it making you feel better? By saying you want to fix things for someone with a disability, consider what you are implying. Disability is not wrong and doesn't need to be fixed.

---

[14]Gina Rippon's The Gendered Brain is a great place to start.

There are many horror stories of software made worse in the name of accessibility and disabled users who are expected to be grateful.[15] Be careful not to use empathy as a reason to act but a reason to investigate. Empathy is not a replacement for real experience; someone's lived experience should guide you more than any feeling or guideline. Interaction designer Marie Van Driessche offers this advice:

> *Ask people with disabilities to be at your table. Most people are not interested in talking to disabled people, they prefer to empathize. But empathy is not helping us.*
>
> —Marie van Driessche[16]

People with disabilities want to have an equivalent experience. They want to be able to use your app just as anyone else does. Accessibility is not a gesture to make you feel better or to gain your brand influence. Accessibility is a tool to achieve inclusion within your software.

Bias

Unconscious bias is something we all have. It is an entirely natural part of being human that we have evolved as a survival mechanism. As such, to fight against unconscious biases can be counterproductive. Research on unconscious bias training shows that if anything, this makes biases worse and encourages stereotyping.[17]

---

[15]May, Matt. "Design Without Empathy", November 23, 2019. https://accessibility.scot/design-without-empathy/.

[16]van Driessche, Marie. Twitter Post. September 4, 2019, 2:33pm. https://twitter.com/marievandries/status/1169242121108369409.

[17]Duguid, Michelle M., Thomas-Hunt, Melissa C. "Condoning stereotyping? How awareness of stereotyping prevalence impacts expression of stereotypes". Journal of Applied Psychology, 100(2), 343–359. 2015. https://doi.org/10.1037/a0037908

The best option is to acknowledge and accept that we all have biases, and use them to help guide you. Ensure your team is as diverse as possible. This will help your team empathize with as many people as possible by using each other's personal knowledge and experience in the form of your own biases. In this way, you can build up a broader base to examine the consequences of the decisions made in your software.

Move Fast and Break Things

Overall, I would like us to finally put to bed the philosophy that has caused a whole lot of bad in software – "Move fast and break things." Even Mark Zuckerberg[18] himself seems to now be realizing this is not a legitimate way of operating anything, let alone a consumer-focused business. I want to propose a new philosophy we can use to make software, one where we work in a considered and empathetic manner to progressively improve the experience for as many people as possible.

Summary

- Inclusive thinking has its root in industrial design and architecture. But this doesn't mean its guiding principles don't apply to engineering too.

- Accessibility is about inclusion. Make changes that will bring your customer into your app rather than making a separate experience for people with different abilities. Allow your customers to customize their experience to suit them.

---

[18]Statt, Nick. "Zuckerberg: 'Move fast and break things' isn't how Facebook operates anymore", CNET, April 30, 2014. www.cnet.com/news/zuckerberg-move-fast-and-break-things-isnt-how-we-operate-anymore/.

- Remember who your users are; they're not always going to be like you, your colleagues, friends, or family. User testing is an essential tool to find out how people experience your app. Make sure your participants are varied.

- Empathy is an essential quality of any software engineer. It helps you to remember to treat your users as unique individuals.

We now have a background on what accessibility and inclusion mean and what has driven thinking in these fields. Let's begin to look at practical ways we can help different people who want to use our apps. Before we cover any specific technologies, we should look at what our aims are. The Web Content Accessibility Guidelines, or WCAG, form a definitive framework on what improvements we should make to our apps to make them more accessible.

CHAPTER 3

Web Content Accessibility Guidelines for Mobile

With a name like Web Content Accessibility Guidelines, it can be tempting to write these off as not applicable to mobile. The name, however, is a function of the era the guidelines were authored throughout the 1990s and 2000s, with the last major update coming in 2008, a time before mobile enjoyed the ubiquity it does today. This is combined with the fact that the initiative comes from the World Wide Web Consortium. The name is also somewhat of a mouthful, so we'll stick with the common acronym of WCAG.

WCAG[1] has been developed with input from a wide range of accessibility professionals, researchers, and users. Like any set of guidelines, it can feel like conforming to WCAG is a checkbox exercise. Accessibility is indeed all about how people experience your app. But unless you have the resources to test extensively with large numbers of users of varied assistive technologies, the WCAG guidelines are by far the best guide you will get.

W3C has split the WCAG into four layers. They begin with four overarching *principles* – perceivable, operable, understandable, and

---

[1]https://www.w3.org/TR/WCAG21/

© Rob Whitaker 2020
R. Whitaker, *Developing Inclusive Mobile Apps*,
https://doi.org/10.1007/978-1-4842-5814-9_3

robust. These principles each have *guidelines,* followed by *success criteria* and *techniques.* Recommendations were initially written expressly for the Web. But the majority of the *principles* and *guidelines* are generic and do translate to mobile, even if their *success criteria* and *techniques* for compliance don't always. The most recent version, WCAG 2.1, was ratified in 2018 and does cover more mobile-related matters such as screen orientation.

WCAG, an ISO standard since 2012, forms the basis of many accessibility laws throughout the world. It is often used as the benchmark for courts to decide if a digital experience is accessible or otherwise for the sake of accessibility lawsuits. As such, so far as the law is concerned, WCAG very much applies to mobile.

In this chapter, I won't cover each guideline in full; for that, I would recommend reading the current WCAG 2.1 specification yourself, available at `www.w3.org/TR/WCAG21`. Instead, I will offer some general advice on how to conform to each guideline on mobile and what tools you might use to do this. We cover each of these techniques and tools in more detail later in the book. In short, I have attempted to take the web-focused *success criteria* and *techniques* and translate them into a mobile context. W3C's detailed guidance for the Web comes to a far greater number of pages than that of this book, so I will keep to a high level for the sake of brevity. W3Cs Web Accessibility Initiative guides on applying WCAG to mobile[2] but somewhat confusingly includes very definitely nonmobile devices such as airplane seatbacks and household appliances in their advice. For the most part, where the WCAG guidelines refer to "web pages" we can assume this includes mobile app content.

---

[2]`www.w3.org/WAI/standards-guidelines/mobile/`

Perceivable

Information and user interface components must be presentable to users in ways they can perceive.

—WCAG 2.1

The first principle, perceivable, covers the content in your application and ways in which you make that available to your customer. To summarize this principle in a word, I would use "alternatives."

Recall our discussion of the telephone in Chapter 1; the telephone, as initially designed, uses just one medium, audio. While this will cover the majority of use cases, it immediately rules out people who struggle to speak and people who struggle to hear. The invention of the TDD was a necessary alternative to allow people in that situation to have the same experience as the rest of us. In the same vein, if you provide content in a visual-only format such as images, text that is not available to the screen reader, or a captioned video without an audio track, your customers with visual impairments will not be able to access this content.

Text Alternatives

Provide text alternatives for any non-text content so that it can be changed into other forms people need, such as large print, braille, speech, symbols or simpler language.

—WCAG 2.1

Ensure that all non-text content has an appropriate and equivalent text alternative. Often this applies to meaningful images. The distinction between content and noncontent is essential here. Providing a descriptive accessible label to decorative images can give a richer experience for your users. But be careful not to distract from your app's content.

53

The ability to add a text alternative to almost any object is baked into both platforms. We cover each option in detail in the iOS Accessibility Model and Android Accessibility Model chapters. Android uses the contentDescription property (Listing 3-1 and Listing 3-2). In iOS, accessibilityLabel will achieve the same (Listing 3-3). Each of these approaches has implementation details; see Chapter 4 and Chapter 6 for more.

Listing 3-1. Setting an Android contentDescription in a layout XML file

```
<Button
    ...
    android:contentDescription="Submit" />
```

Listing 3-2. Setting an Android contentDescription in code

```
submitButton.contentDescription = "Submit"
```

Listing 3-3. Setting an accessibility label in iOS

```
submitButton.accessibilityLabel = "Submit"
```

ALTERNATIVE TEXT FOR IMAGES

Images that have a UI function, such as a button, must have a clear, descriptive text alternative label so that screen reader users can know there is an action available and what the consequences of this action will be.

Decorative images require more consideration. Small decorative images such as icons drawing attention to content in a table row should probably not contain alternative text. This adds unnecessary noise, increases the number of swipes required to navigate, and confuses your UI order resulting in your user losing context.

Larger decorative images such as hero images, however, probably should contain a text description of the purpose of the image – for example, an icon of a tick should contain the description "you're all set" rather than "tick icon." This label should never take focus away from the page header but, instead, serve as an indication to partially sighted screen reader users who are trying to locate themselves on the screen. If the screen reader skips a large area of a screen, these users may assume this part of the screen includes content you have not made fully accessible and will attempt to locate any content in this area. This will result in an annoying "dunk" sound on iOS if you fail to describe what's present. Think of this as the screen reader equivalent of "This page is left intentionally blank."

Time-Based Media

Provide alternatives for time-based media.

—WCAG 2.1

To you and I, this means audio and video. Additionally, it covers any media that has a time component to it such as animation. Video and audio should feature captions or a transcription. Preferably video should include audio description, and ideally both audio and video should incorporate or have an option for sign language. More details on captions and alternative tracks for media are available in Chapters 5 and 10.

This guideline excludes video or audio you provide as an alternative to text. If you do provide these as an alternative, be sure to mark them as such. If you don't make it evident to you users that your media is an alternative, people who can't use this may feel excluded.

Adaptable

Create content that can be presented in different ways (for example simpler layout) without losing information or structure.

—WCAG 2.1

The adaptable guideline moves away from the content and covers how you present the content in your UI.

Present content in a clear, meaningful order. You can achieve this through good interface design, but take care to test with screen readers enabled. These can often navigate your screen in ways that might not be natural to sighted users. For example, consider a screen with a large hero image followed by a title. Your eye would usually skim the image and be drawn to the title. A screen reader will focus on the alt text given to your image first unless you specify that the title should be the initially focused item.

Present information in multiple sensory characteristics. Don't rely on color alone, for example, but a combination of attributes such as color, shape, size, location, or sound. You can use any or all of these modes together to infer meaning.

Input fields and other controls should identify the purpose or action for that control. Use the `contentDescription` property on Android and `accessibilityLabel` property on iOS we previously discussed to achieve this. On iOS, accessibility traits are a powerful tool to inform assistive technology, and its users, about how a control will function. An `accessibilityHint` on iOS (Listing 3-5) or `hint` on Android (Listing 3-4) can give extra context if needed. Chapter 4 on the Android Accessibility Model and Chapter 6 on the iOS Accessibility Model provide more detail on how to use these.

Listing 3-4. Setting a hint in an Android layout XML file

```
<EditText
...
android:hint="Email Address" />
```

Listing 3-5. Setting an accessibility hint in UIKit

```
sendButton.accessibilityHint = "Sends your message."
```

PROVIDING HINTS

When using descriptions, labels, or hints to provide context, it can be tempting to give a little too much background, for example, adding "double tap to edit" as a hint on a text field.

Remember: Screen reader users will be just as natural at using a screen reader interface as you or I may be at using a visual interface. While these differences in navigation may be new to you, there's no need to explain them. Doing so adds unnecessary noise and may appear patronizing to your users.

A new addition for WCAG 2.1 is a result of the rising popularity of mobile. User interfaces should not be constrained into one orientation but should allow rotation into any device-supported orientation. This applies unless an explicit orientation is a requirement for a defined purpose, such as requiring landscape for a musical keyboard.

Distinguishable

Make it easier for users to see and hear content including separating foreground from background.

—WCAG 2.1

The distinguishable guideline covers how your users tell the difference between elements in your app. This guideline includes essential rules for contrast, text size and line spacing, background audio, and others. Some disabilities such as color blindness might impede our ability to distinguish between elements. So sticking to these guides and allowing customizability, where needed, are essential. Unless your layout demands it, avoid scrolling in two dimensions as this can be a trigger for people sensitive to movement. It can be challenging to control with some assistive technologies enabled.

This guideline also provides advice on the following elements.

Color

Your use of color in any app is crucial. The right choice of palette can be a significant factor in setting your app apart. Well-used color can be a subtle hint at meaning and aid understanding. Remember, however, that not everyone's experience of color is the same; therefore, the color should never be the only way to identify elements or convey meaning. Combine coloring with text, shapes, or animation. Yellow warning triangles, for example, are not just called "yellow warnings" – the triangle part is essential to its utility.

The contrast ratio between your text color and the text's background color are a material consideration. Large text – defined as a minimum of 18pt, or 14pt bold – should have a minimum contrast ratio of 3:1. Smaller text should have a contrast ratio of 4.5:1. Ideally, your text should have a contrast ratio of 7:1, with larger text at 4.5:1. We cover checking your color contrast ratios in Chapter 11.

Some people, such as those experiencing dyslexia, Irlen syndrome, or color blindness, can benefit from the ability to customize background colors. This would be a great addition to your app if you're looking to take your accessibility to the next level.

Audio

Any audio in your app, including audio as part of video, lasting longer than 3 seconds should have controls. These should allow for pausing, stopping, and adjusting the volume. The volume control should be independent of the system control to let your customer maintain their chosen system level.

Any speech audio should avoid background sounds. Alternatively, allow the disabling of background sounds or have background sounds a minimum of 20db (at least four times) quieter than the speech audio. Background noise can affect those with attention disorders; it can also make the foreground audio challenging to determine for some people with hearing impairments if their hearing is distorted.

Text

Text should be resizable up to double the glyph size without losing content or functionality. Ensuring you support system, dynamic text sizes on both platforms will fulfil this requirement. Avoid using images of text as these don't support screen readers or text size adjustments. If you must use an image containing text, ensure you add a screen reader-accessible label including the text to the image. Do this using the `contentDescription` property on Android or `accessibilityLabel` on iOS.

When formatting text, aim for the following: avoid full justification, keep lines of text to a maximum of 80 characters, and provide paragraph spacing of 1.5 times the line spacing. Let your users customize to their needs by providing a mechanism to change text and background colors.

Operable

> *User interface components and navigation must be operable.*
>
> —WCAG 2.1

As the name for this principle suggests, operable covers how your app works. This includes working with any assistive technology your customer may choose to use as an alternative input or output mechanism.

Keyboard Accessible

Make all functionality available from a keyboard.

—WCAG 2.1

Ensure your app is navigable using an external keyboard. Make sure your app is free of keyboard traps – a control that can be focused by the keyboard but will only lose focus by another means. The equivalent can also happen when navigating the interface using screen readers. Be sure to browse to each control with both screen readers and external keyboards enabled when testing your app.

Both platforms support keyboard navigation, but each's implementations are lacking in different ways. See Chapters 5 and 12 for more on this.

Time Limits

Provide users enough time to read and use content.

—WCAG 2.1

Time limits can be desirable for many reasons: to free products or resources preventing denial of service attack or added security for your users by restricting unauthorized use of authorization tokens. However, time limits can create a barrier for some people. Navigating an app with assistive technology can be time-consuming, especially if the accessible design is not up to standard. Additionally, people with anxiety disorders can find time limits very pressuring.

Where possible, avoid time limits if there is no strict requirement for one. If you do include a time limit, consider providing a mechanism for your user to choose the limit or to extend it. Warn before a limit is about to expire, and give an option to reset or extend. If reauthentication is required, allow your customer to pick up where they left off before their authentication expired.

Additionally, this guideline provides rules on moving, blinking scrolling, or auto-updating content. Provide a mechanism to pause, stop or hide these at the request of the user.

Seizures and Physical Reactions

Do not design content in a way that is known to cause seizures or physical reactions.

—WCAG 2.1

Any flashing or blinking present should not flash more than three times a second. This is known to cause physical reactions in people with epilepsy. Additionally, you should provide the option for your customer to disable animation unless this is essential to the functionality of your app. On iOS, you should listen to the `isReduceMotionEnabled` property.

Navigable

Provide ways to help users navigate, find content, and determine where they are.

—WCAG 2.1

Assuming here that you are a sighted user, when greeted with a page of content, your eyes and brain work together subconsciously to build a mental model of what's available to you. This unconscious technique allows you to instantaneously skip between content to find what's most important to you right now. For this reason, digital advertising tries to be as distracting as possible. If the adverts weren't distracting, your brain would likely judge it unimportant and skip past without you even realizing you had done so. If you're not fully sighted, this is a tool you're unable to benefit from. You'll rely on extra clues to augment yourself with the content.

It's crucial to ensure screen readers and other assistive technologies can navigate your app in a logical order, making sure content is separated with meaningful titles. At times, the navigation order for screen readers can differ from the order your eyes may be naturally drawn. It is possible to achieve correct, semantic, screen reader order in many ways. Setting some elements hidden to the screen reader, adjusting content order or primary focus for the screen reader, or by the use of semantic views are all techniques to achieve this. We'll cover each later in the book.

Each screen should have a title accessible to the screen reader, and you should mark any content headings as such. This allows screen reader users to skip through meaningful headings in an analogy to the skim reading we discussed above.

You should strive for all your buttons to have unique, meaningful text labels, ones that don't require any additional context to be useful.

Input Modalities

> *Make it easier for users to operate functionality through various inputs beyond keyboard.*
>
> —WCAG 2.1

If your app makes use of the device's built-in accelerometer to determine movement and control features of your app, provide an alternative for people who may struggle with fine motor control.

Tap targets should be a minimum of 44 pixels square. Android's guidelines recommend a minimum of 48px square. Anything smaller will be challenging to press accurately and will result in accidental input and customer frustration.

This guideline also covers touch gestures that can be used to control features in your app. Consider that it may not be possible for all users to perform your prescribed gesture accurately, so offer alternatives. iOS allows you to mark your elements (not limited to buttons) as having accessibility actions. These can be triggered by your user directly using their assistive technology.

Understandable

Information and the operation of user interface must be understandable.

—WCAG 2.1

WCAG's third principle – understandable – aims to improve the clarity of your app and its functionality. This principle covers content, design, and the behavior of your app.

Readable

Make text content readable and understandable.

—WCAG 2.1

Avoid idioms, jargon, and abbreviations in your text where possible. For any you do use, offer a mechanism for your user to determine their definition. Ideally, aim for any written content to be understandable at a lower secondary education level.[3]

---

[3]For guidance on tailoring your language, see www.plainlanguage.gov/ guidelines/ for US English and www.plainenglish.co.uk/free-guides.html for UK English.

Predictable

Make Web pages appear and operate in predictable ways.

—WCAG 2.1

Consistency in design and operation is vital for this guideline. No two identical-looking controls should function differently. The inverse is also true; two controls with the same function should have the same appearance.

Any changes of context – moving or changing the meaning or behavior of controls or content such as navigating to a new screen – should not happen without warning. These should only occur at the request of the user, by, say, pressing a button. Or you should inform your customer that something will happen, perhaps with a loading spinner. Failure to prepare a user for a change of context can cause anxiety for some customers with mental health problems or learning difficulties. Additionally, visually impaired users may not be aware that context has changed, thus making the meaning of the new content unclear.

Input Assistance

Help users avoid and correct mistakes.

—WCAG 2.1

When collecting data from your customer through a form, any errors should be highlighted clearly in position. Provide an indication of what is causing the error and how this can be rectified. Each field should provide clear instructions to your user as to their purpose.

Ideally, any forms should provide at least one of the following features:

- Reversible
  It is possible to reverse the submission of data.

- Checked
  Data entered is validated before submission. Your customer is provided with an opportunity to correct any errors.

- Confirmed
  Provide your customer with the opportunity to review, confirm, and correct any data entered before finalizing their submission.

Robust

Content must be robust enough that it can be interpreted by ...assistive technologies.

—WCAG 2.1

The final principle contains just one guideline. The essential rule is that your app should be compatible with any assistive technology available on your user's chosen platform.

Compatible

Maximize compatibility with current and future ...assistive technologies.

—WCAG 2.1

The purpose of your controls should be determinable by your user's chosen assistive technology. You can achieve this using accessibility traits on iOS. For example, any control that acts as a button should be marked as such. This allows the assistive technology in use to make a decision on how to behave for that element.

Summary

- The World Wide Web Consortium's Web Content Accessibility Guidelines set out rules for how you should measure the accessibility of your app.

- It's an international standard and forms the legal framework for deciding whether your app is accessible. If you don't meet the criteria in WCAG, you're at risk of legal disputes. If you're concerned, get a WCAG expert to review your app and determine which guidelines apply to you and how.

- WCAG is the result of well-resourced research from users and experts, people who really do understand what's best for accessibility. Use the result of their extensive experience to guide you.

- Your app should be perceivable, operable, understandable, and robust.

We've covered the background of what considerations you should make to improve your app's accessibility and briefly covered why you should make them. Let's now move on to the tools each platform provides you to conform with these guidelines. First, we'll start with Android.

CHAPTER 4

Android Accessibility Model

As is the case with the rest of the platform, Android accessibility is highly customizable. A large part of accessibility is about customizability, so Android has a huge edge here. If Android doesn't have a system setting that suits a specific need, then any developer can create a custom accessibility service to fulfil that need. We'll take a cursory look at this in the "Viewing the accessibility tree" activity later. Because of the wide variation in handsets and software versions available, for the avoidance of doubt, I'm using a Google Pixel device running Android 10.

Google's design system Material Design[1] runs throughout Android system apps and is the basis for the apps you create. Google developed Material Design with high standards of accessibility in mind and following the best practices of user interface design. Using Android's inbuilt controls (Figure 4-1)[2] and following Material Design principles will mean your app

---

[1]https://material.io
[2]https://material.io/components/

© Rob Whitaker 2020
R. Whitaker, *Developing Inclusive Mobile Apps*,
https://doi.org/10.1007/978-1-4842-5814-9_4

is consistent – not only consistent with the Android system but with the rest of your app.[3] This will help all your users to feel at home when using your app and help you maintain a high level of accessibility.

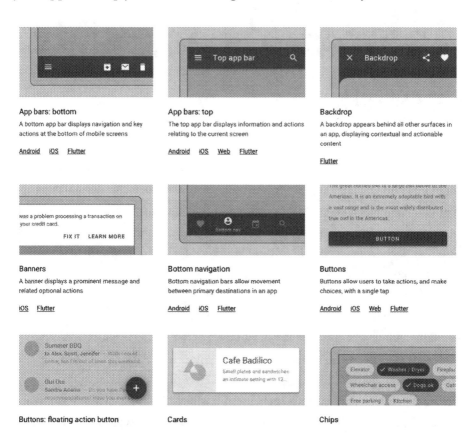

Figure 4-1. *Material Design components from material.io*

---

[3]Google has also made Material Design available for iOS, but this is the wrong type of consistency. Using Material Design on iOS means a far greater context switch for users when entering/leaving your app. Using Material Design on iOS will result in a less accessible app. Google warns against this in Material Design's accessibility guidelines, at the same time as encouraging Material Design's use on iOS. ☺

Material design's guidelines are a great introduction to using Android's tools to create an accessible experience. Take a read through Google's introduction on Material Design principles[4] and Material Design accessibility[5] for best practices. Most of the information in the Material Design guide is relevant to anyone making Android apps, not only designers.

Accessibility Tree

Before we cover the accessibility features available on Android, let's cover how the Android accessibility model works for assistive technologies. When using an Android app, you'll be familiar with the controls and views that Android inflates from XML. Creating a user interface you can interact with. But how are these visual elements translated into a format that assistive technologies can use?

Android creates what is known as an accessibility tree, a hierarchical representation of elements that are present on the screen. Assistive services can use this accessibility tree to determine how to present information. Android makes some reasonable assumptions about your user interface and how to represent it to assistive technology. Most of the time, this will give a functioning accessible experience. At times you may need to tweak this tree to present a better experience. This chapter will provide you with the tools and techniques to do this.

---

[4]https://material.io/design/introduction/
[5]https://material.io/design/usability/accessibility.html

Accessibility Nodes

Android provides data to accessibility services in the form of a tree of accessibility nodes. Accessibility nodes are representations of elements on the screen. They contain content and metadata about the element and actions that assistive technology can perform.

The distinction between an accessibility node and an on-screen element is crucial. Android doesn't present assistive technologies with the on-screen element but a proxy object containing information that is relevant to accessibility. Once the accessibility service receives a node, this node is immutable. Changes to the view are not revealed to the accessibility service until next time the service requests the node.

The accessibility node contains information about the element that is useful to assistive technology, for example, properties like text and description, information such as if an element is scrollable or a heading is also included. So are details of the element's position on screen and it's hierarchy.

VIEWING THE ACCESSIBILITY TREE

Android allows any developer to create an accessibility service. This service can be used to present content on the screen, control the screen or device, or any other task you might expect of an assistive technology. We won't cover the ins and outs of making such a service in this book, although Android does provide a guide on doing this.[6] We will touch on the basics as a way of illustrating how the accessibility tree works.

If you haven't already, clone the GitHub repo for this book. Navigate to the folder Exercise 4-1. Open this example code in Android Studio, and click Run.

---

[6]https://developer.android.com/guide/topics/ui/accessibility/service

On your device or emulator, open Settings and find Accessibility. At the top here, you should see your new accessibility service listed under Downloaded Services (Figure 4-2). Open the service, and enable it.

DOWNLOADED SERVICES

uk.co.rwapp.accessibilitytree.AccessibilityTr
ee
Off

Figure 4-2. *Our new accessibility service in our device's accessibility settings*

The accessibility service will overlay a "Get Accessibility Tree" button at the top of your screen (Figure 4-3).

Figure 4-3. *"Get Accessibility Tree" button overlayed at the top of our screen*

Open the Logcat tab in Android Studio. Click the new "Get Accessibility Tree" button. You'll see a bunch of output printed (Figure 4-4). These are the text descriptions and labels of all of the current elements on the screen. Try navigating to different screens, and click the button again to see what is presented to the accessibility service with different layouts.

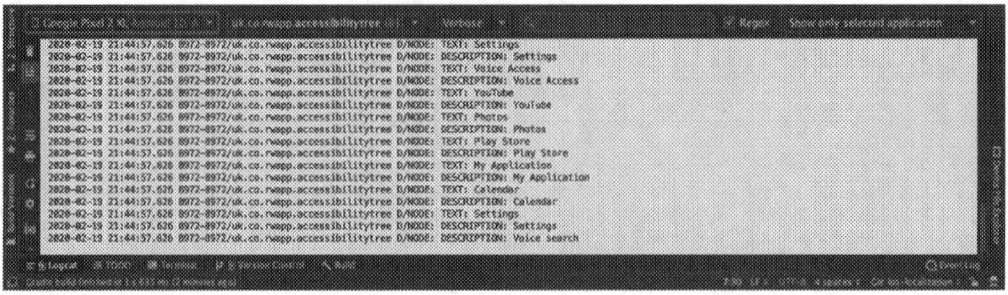

Figure 4-4. *Accessibility tree output from the Android app launcher*

For the full list of properties available to accessibility services, check the Android documentation.[7] Consider querying different values (Listing 4-1) such as isHeading to see how each screen reports itself for accessibility. For example, see the following listing.

Listing 4-1. Printing to the console if an element is clickable

```
if (node.isClickable) {
    Log.d("NODE", "is Clickable")
}
```

Accessibility API

Android's accessibility APIs are responsible for managing the views presented to accessibility services. Google has made some reasonable assumptions when creating their standard controls. Stick with Android classes for controls, and your accessibility will be okay. But there will be times you'll need to make tweaks to improve what we present to accessibility users. This is especially true when you create your own

---

[7]https://developer.android.com/reference/android/view/accessibility/ AccessibilityNodeInfo.html

custom controls. If you change Android's built-in controls, it's essential you check you haven't removed any accessibility features. We'll take a look at some of the properties you might need to consider setting here.

Content Description

For an assistive technology like TalkBack to present an element to your user, the technology needs a textual representation to present. The contentDescription is set to your view's text value by default. For elements with no text value, or where the text value would not work when presented by assistive tech, you should set the contentDescription value (Listing 4-2 and Listing 4-3).

contentDescription should be a concise, descriptive label. Often one word is plenty, such as "Submit." Don't include the type of control such as "button" as Android will add this for you. Don't repeat descriptions, keeping these unique aids navigation.

Listing 4-2. Setting a contentDescription in a layout XML file

```
<Button
    ...
    android:contentDescription="Submit" />
```

Listing 4-3. Setting a contentDescription in code

```
submitButton.contentDescription = "Submit"
```

As with all properties that can be set in a layout file, this value can also be set in the Attributes pane when in design mode as in Figure 4-5.

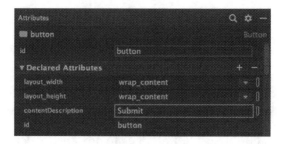

Figure 4-5. *Changing a property in the Attributes pane*

Important for Accessibility

If an element is purely decorative such as an icon accompanying text, adding this element to your accessibility tree means extra unnecessary swipes for TalkBack users. In this case, we shouldn't provide this element to assistive technologies. You can do this by setting `importantForAccessibility` to no (Listing 4-4 and Listing 4-5). Alternatively, if an element that is usually hidden provides context, you can set the value to yes.

Listing 4-4. Setting a view inaccessible in XML

```
<TextView
    ...
    android:importantForAccessibility="no" />
```

Listing 4-5. Setting a view inaccessible in code

```
textIcon.importantForAccessibility =
    IMPORTANT_FOR_ACCESSIBILITY_NO
```

Hint

A hint value is a text representation of an element separate to the element's text value (Listing 4-6). These values are used in different ways by Android, depending on if your element has another text value or not.

For an element without a text value, the hint is displayed as a placeholder value. The hint is also read by TalkBack as the text label. This is useful for `EditText` elements to provide users with a prompt for what information they should enter. For these purposes, your hint should be short and descriptive, following the same queues as for the `contentDescription` above.

For elements with a text value, the hint is not displayed. TalkBack reads the hint after the elements text value or `contentDescription` and element type. You can use a hint to provide more context to your user if it helps them navigate your UI. An ideal use would be to give a short description of the consequence of pressing a button, for example. A button with the text "send" might have the hint of "Sends your message." This makes it explicit what action will be performed and what the expected result is. As a general guide for writing hints, imagine explaining to a friend what this control does.

Listing 4-6. Setting a hint in a layout XML file

```
<EditText
    ...
    android:hint="Email Address" />
```

Accessibility Heading

When navigating a screen with TalkBack, users who have no, or very little, eyesight navigate by swiping from left to right over the screen. TalkBack focuses on each element on screen in order, from top left to bottom right. For screens with a large amount of content, this can mean a lot of swiping through irrelevant content for your customer to find the information they're looking for. Marking your headings as such (Listing 4-7 and Listing 4-8) allows TalkBack users to skim headings skipping content.

Listing 4-7. Setting an element as a heading in a layout XML file

```
<TextView
    ...
    android:accessibilityHeading="true" />
```

Listing 4-8. Setting an element as a heading in code

```
headingLabel.isAccessibilityHeading = true
```

Minimum Size

All interactive elements, such as buttons, checkboxes, switches, and other controls, must be a minimum of 44 relative pixels square to meet WCAG guidelines. Android recommends using a minimum of 48 relative pixels.

Android provides a simple way to ensure this is always the case. This will be maintained regardless of the device or the rest of your UI. Set `minWidth` and `minHeight` values against any interactive controls (Listing 4-9 and Listing 4-10). Get into the habit of making this a standard property for any control you add to your UI.

Listing 4-9. Setting a minimum size for an image button in XML

```
<ImageButton
    ...
    android:minHeight="48dp"
    android:minWidth="48dp" />
```

Listing 4-10. Setting a minimum size for an image button in Kotlin

```
imageButton.minWidth = 48
imageButton.minHeight = 48
```

Label For

Say we're presenting a form to our customer with some EditText field for them to fill in. How does our customer know what data to enter in which field? One common way to do this is to add a hint value to our EditText. Android displays this as a placeholder for the field (Figure 4-6).

Figure 4-6. *EditText control with a hint (left) and the same control with content (right). Note with content the hint is hidden*

This works fine when the field is unpopulated. Once the field has a value entered, this placeholder disappears (Figure 4-6), and it's no longer clear what the purpose of this field is. This is a bad experience for people who may struggle with attention or memory. labelFor allows us to tie a TextView element to an EditText or other control. This label remains visible regardless of the state of the control (Figure 4-7). Unfortunately, this technique does add extra unneeded swipes for TalkBack users, but on balance, I believe using the labelFor property will benefit more of your customers than it will inconvenience.

Figure 4-7. *EditText control with an associated label (left). The label stays visible even when content is entered (right)*

The labelFor property is set on the TextView that is the "label for" the control provided as an argument (Listing 4-11 and Listing 4-12). Provide the id of the view to which you want to tie this label.

Listing 4-11. Setting a text label for an edit text control in XML

```
<LinearLayout
    ...
    >
    <TextView
        ...
        android:layout_marginBottom="0dp"
        android:labelFor="@+id/editText"
        android:text="@string/name" />
    <EditText
        ...
        android:id="@+id/editText"
        android:layout_marginTop="0dp"
        android:text="" />
</LinearLayout>
```

Listing 4-12. Setting a label for an EditText control in Kotlin

```
textView.labelFor = editText.id
```

Traversal Order

The accessibility tree is built in natural reading order. This means the order that TalkBack and other assistive technologies will move from the top-left-most item to the bottom-right-most item. This is generally the correct behavior. But some designs such as staggered elements can read differently to how a visual user might read them. An example of this sort of layout can be seen in the Google Play Store, where an app's download numbers are presented directly vertically under the heading of "downloads."

In this situation, we might want to improve our accessibility tree by telling Android which element should come next or previous when an accessibility service navigates our UI. Android features two different ways of specifying traversal order depending on the type of technology your customer is using. If you find the traversal order Android determines for you is not ideal, then we need to be sure we set both of these options.

Accessibility Traversal Order

We can do this using the `accessibilityTraversalAfter` and `accessibilityTraversalBefore` properties. Personally, I find it challenging to understand the behavior of these properties from their names. The element on which you are setting this property is the element "before" and "after" are referring to. Let's illustrate this in Figure 4-8 to clarify the meaning.

Figure 4-8. *Three buttons. We want to ensure they are navigated in numerical order*

Consider we have three buttons. We'll label them "1," "2," and "3" for clarity. We want to guarantee these elements are traversed in the correct numerical ascending order. To do this, we would set after and before values on 2. 2's `accessibilityTraversalBefore` value would be 1, because we want 1 to be traversed *before* 2. So that makes 2's `accessibilityTraversalAfter` value 3, as we want 3 to come *after* 2. The XML to create this can be seen in Listing 4-13.

Listing 4-13. Setting accessibility traversal order in XML

```
<Button
    ...
    android:id="@+id/button1"
    android:text="@string/one" />

<Button
    ...
    android:id="@+id/button2"
    android:accessibilityTraversalAfter="@id/ button3"
    android:accessibilityTraversalBefore="@id/ button1"
    android:text="@string/two" />

<Button
    ...
    android:id="@+id/button3"
    android:text="@string/three" />
```

You can also set these in code with the `setAccessibilityTraversal After()` and `setAccessibilityTraversalBefore()` methods and passing the `id` of the view you want to visit before/next as in Listing 4-14.

Listing 4-14. Setting accessibility traversal order in Kotlin

```
two.setAccessibilityTraversalAfter(one.id)
two.setAccessibilityTraversalBefore(three.id)
```

Directional Control

In accessibility traversal order, we need to set focus order. Focus order is used by Android when users navigate your UI with a directional pad, remote, or keyboard arrow keys. We set these on an element to specify which element should be next focused when a customer presses a key in the particular direction. The properties are nextFocusDown, nextFocusUp, nextFocusLeft, and nextFocusRight for handling arrow key input and nextFocusForward for tab input.

Figure 4-9. *A grid of nine buttons. We want to ensure directional navigation works as expected from the number 5*

For this example, let's say we have a 3 by 3 grid of elements numbered 1 to 9 (Figure 4-9). What if we're in the center element, number 5? We need to guarantee up will move to 2, down to 8, left to 4, right to 6, and forward also moves to 6. The XML for our center element, number 5, would be the as in Listing 4-15.

Listing 4-15. Setting directional focus in XML

```
<Button
      android:id="@+id/button5"
      android:nextFocusUp="@id/button2"
      android:nextFocusDown="@id/button8"
      android:nextFocusLeft="@id/button4"
      android:nextFocusRight="@id/button6"
      android:nextFocusForward="@id/button6"
      android:text="@string/five" />
```

Or if we need to change this in our app's code (Listing 4-16), we can set these values here too passing the id of the view we want focused next in each direction.

Listing 4-16. Setting directional focus in Kotlin

```
button5.nextFocusUpId(button2.id)
button5.nextFocusDownId(button8.id)
button5.nextFocusLeftId(button4.id)
button5.nextFocusRightId(button6.id)
button5.nextFocusForwardId(button6.id)
```

There is one other consideration that we need to address with directional control. In Android's standard implementation of this feature, the default focus highlight is not easily distinguishable (Figure 4-10), meaning we have to add our own.

Figure 4-10. *Keyboard navigation highlighting the date – you likely can't tell there is a box around the date*

The best way to do this is to override the `colorControlHighlight` for your app's theme in your styles.xml file as in Listing 4-17.

Listing 4-17. Setting our app's theme's control highlight color to our accent color

```
<style name="AppTheme" parent="Theme.MaterialComponents.DayNight">
    ...
    <item name="android:colorControlHighlight">@color/
            colorAccent</item>
</style>
```

Custom Controls

If you stick with using Android's provided controls within your app, Android will handle accessibility events for you. If you want to customize a control, take the existing control closest to what you want to achieve and build on top. Sometimes though you have little choice but to build a control from the ground up. Although it is not recommended from an accessibility perspective, for complex elements, this is sometimes required. If you chose to do this, it's essential to test your control with different accessibility services thoroughly.

To begin, you'll need to ensure you have implemented the majority of the properties featured in this chapter. Once you have set these values, Android provides thorough documentation on other functions you may need to override on your control.[8] Which methods you need to implement will depend on your control, but we'll cover some of the most important here.

Accessibility Actions

The `AccessibilityNodeInfo` is also the place we need to tell Android about the actions assistive technology can perform on our view. It is an opportunity for us to give our customer more information about what our control is capable of and how.

---

[8]https://developer.android.com/guide/topics/ui/accessibility/custom-views

83

If you focus on a button with TalkBack, TalkBack will read "Double tap to activate" once the element's value has been read. This is an accessibility action, and it's comprised of two parts. The button is telling Android it is capable of an onClick event. From this piece of information, Android adds "Double tap to." Then "activate" is a string provided by the button. We need to mimic this for our own control. Let's say we have a new control that opens a detail view on a tap event and shows a menu of options on a long press. Our code would look like Listing 4-18.

Listing 4-18. Adding accessibility actions to a custom view

```
class MyView: View {

    constructor(context: Context, attrs: AttributeSet):
    super(context, attrs)

    override fun onInitializeAccessibilityNodeInfo
    (info: AccessibilityNodeInfo?) {
        super.onInitializeAccessibilityNodeInfo(info)

        val click = AccessibilityNodeInfo.AccessibilityAction
        (AccessibilityNodeInfo.ACTION_CLICK, "open")

        val longClick = AccessibilityNodeInfo.AccessibilityAction
        (AccessibilityNodeInfo.ACTION_LONG_CLICK, "show options")

        info?.addAction(click)
        info?.addAction(longClick)
    }
}
```

Event Handling

While adding a setOnClickListener() to a view may make it function correctly when our customer taps the screen, it doesn't guarantee that your view will respond to Voice Access, TalkBack, or other accessibility services correctly. You should test whether you need to override the sendAccessibilityEvent() or sendAccessibilityEventUnchecked() functions. These methods are fired every time an accessibility event is triggered on your view, including focusing and tapping.

Depending on how your view is created, Android may already handle activation events for you as you would expect. For events like focusing on an element with an accessible service, you may need to make a change to your view, such as adding a highlight. You could do this by checking if an event is related to the accessibility focus as in Listing 4-19.

Listing 4-19. Setting the background color of a view red when it receives accessibility focus. Black when focus leaves the view

```
class MyView: View {

    constructor(context: Context, attrs: AttributeSet):
    super(context, attrs)

    override fun sendAccessibilityEvent(eventType: Int) {
        super.sendAccessibilityEvent(eventType)

        when (eventType) {
            AccessibilityEvent.TYPE_VIEW_ACCESSIBILITY_FOCUS_
            CLEARED ->
                background = Color.BLACK.toDrawable()

            AccessibilityEvent.TYPE_VIEW_FOCUSED ->
                background =
                Color.RED.toDrawable()
        }
    }
}
```

Text Changed Event

Whenever the text value of your control changes, accessibility services need to know about this. This helps Android ensure that what is presented to an accessibility user is the same as displayed on the screen. To do this, your custom view must inform Android the value has changed by posting an accessibility event of TYPE_VIEW_TEXT_CHANGED (Listing 4-20).

Listing 4-20. Informing accessibility about a text change on our custom view

```
sendAccessibilityEvent(AccessibilityEvent.TYPE_VIEW_TEXT_CHANGED)
```

Node Information

To know how to present your view to an accessibility user, Android collects information about your view and its current status. This includes the size and position of the view. When Android requests this information, it calls onInitializeAccessibilityNodeInfo() on your view, passing an initialized AccessibilityNodeInfo for you to populate (Listing 4-21). You should always call super here to let Android fill out some sensible defaults. Then you can add any further attributes your control requires. This could include attributes such as isHeading or isCheckable.

Listing 4-21. Adding properties to our custom view's accessibility info

```
class MyView: View {

    constructor(context: Context, attrs: AttributeSet):
    super(context, attrs)

    override fun onInitializeAccessibilityNodeInfo(info:
    AccessibilityNodeInfo?) {
        super.onInitializeAccessibilityNodeInfo(info)
```

```
        // Accessibility services will treat your view as
           toggleable.
      info?.isCheckable = true
   }
}
```

Delegate

If you are choosing to use the provided Android controls but would like
more fine-grained control over how accessibility works for each, you
can use an AccessibilityDelegate class. Create a class that extends
AccessibilityDelegate; then set this as the delegate on your view
(Listing 4-22). The delegate can override the same accessibility methods
we've covered earlier.

Listing 4-22. Setting an accessibility delegate

```
class MyAccessibilityDelegate : View.AccessibilityDelegate() {

    override fun onInitializeAccessibilityNodeInfo(host: View,
       info: AccessibilityNodeInfo) {
       super.onInitializeAccessibilityNodeInfo(host, info)

       // add custom actions
    }
}

class MyActivity : Activity() {

    override fun onCreate(savedInstanceState: Bundle?) {
       super.onCreate(savedInstanceState)
       setContentView(R.layout.my_activity)

       val accessibilityDelegate = MyAccessibilityDelegate()

       button.accessibilityDelegate = accessibilityDelegate
       }
}
```

Semantic Views

Creating semantic views is a powerful advanced technique for creating the most accessible app you can. A semantic view ties together two or more elements that have a connected meaning. Android then presents them to accessibility users as one element. This reduces the amount of noise and makes navigating your app far more straightforward, faster, and less frustrating. If you are really looking to give your accessibility users the best experience you can, you need to use this technique.

Figure 4-11. *Google Play Store app info*

Google makes use of this technique in the Google Play Store. When looking at a listing page for an app or game, we see three boxes just under the app's icon (Figure 4-11) – the app's rating, number of downloads, and an age rating. The first item, the app's rating, displays "4.4 ★" then on a new line "1K reviews." Additionally, the rating text and the age rating text are buttons. If you access these elements with TalkBack enabled with no changes to the accessibility tree, this is what TalkBack will read:

- "Four point four star. Double tap to activate." Swipe.

- "100 K plus." Swipe.

- "1 K reviews." Swipe.

- "Downloads." Swipe.

- "PEGI 3. Double tap to activate."

That's a lot of swiping. One swipe we only hear the word "downloads." What does 100K refer to? Fortunately, this isn't how TalkBack presents this view. The Google Play Store developers have improved their accessibility tree to provide a better experience. Instead, this is the interaction:

- "Average rating four point four stars in one thousand reviews. Double tap to activate." Swipe.

- "Downloaded 100 thousand plus times." Swipe.

- "Content rating PEGI 3. Double tap to activate."

Grouping these elements together has several benefits. Firstly, fewer swipes are needed, from five down to three. Meaning navigating is faster and simpler. Grouping-related elements like the app review value and the number of reviews provide context to what each value means. The text has also been altered to be more meaningful for TalkBack customers by changing "100 K plus" to "100 thousand plus." While visually it's clear to see the K means thousand, we'd rarely say "k" out loud to mean thousand.

Focusable Containers

One of the simplest ways to achieve this is to use focusable containers. Layout containers such as LinearLayout and RelativeLayout are not visible and contain no content. But they contain properties we can set to make them appear to accessibility services like TalkBack. Consider the app rating from the Google Play Store. If we wanted to achieve something similar, we can use a vertical linear layout as in Listing 4-23.

Listing 4-23. A vertical linear layout with text

```
<LinearLayout
    ...
    android:orientation="vertical">
```

```
<TextView
    ...
    android:text="@string/rating" />
<TextView
    ...
    android:text="@string/number_of_reviews" />
</LinearLayout>
```

Currently, this view requires two swipes for TalkBack navigation, and it might not be clear what the rating value refers to. For clarity, let's make accessibility services see this view as a single element. To do this, we can set the linear layout's focusable property to true. You can do this in code (Listing 4-24) or directly in our XML (Listing 4-25).

Listing 4-24. Setting a linear layout focusable in Kotlin

```
linearLayout.focusable = View.FOCUSABLE
```

Listing 4-25. Setting a linear layout focusable in XML

```
<LinearLayout
    ...
    android:focusable="true"
    android:orientation="vertical">

    ...

</LinearLayout>
```

The result here is for each of the individual text views to no longer appear to TalkBack. Instead, the linear layout is focused, and the Android has passed the text view's values to the linear layout. This is a fabulous improvement, but we still have an issue with the information that is read. Instead of reading "100 thousand reviews," our customer is hearing "100 K reviews." So let's remove the focusable value, and instead pass a content description to the linear layout. We cover how to do this in the Content Description section earlier in this chapter. Instead of just concatenating the two visual strings, generate a new accessible string that makes more sense when read aloud. With a content description, our linear layout has automatically hidden its children. Instead, the layout element is focused, and our new content description read aloud.

Summary

- Android's accessibility services use a technology called an accessibility tree to understand your app's UI. This is built for you, but you need to tweak it to make sure it makes sense for your customers.

- Stick with Android's provided views and controls wherever possible. Accessibility is complicated when creating your own controls. Android has already done much of the hard work for you.

- Group connected views together as semantic views. This will make your app faster to use and easier to understand.

In this chapter, we covered how Android's accessibility system works at a low level. You now have a clearer idea of how to make an interface that is symbiotic with assistive technology. Let's take a closer look at some of the accessibility features Android provides to our customers. We'll also cover some of the decisions we need to make as a developer to best support our users who rely on them.

CHAPTER 5

Android Accessibility Features

In this chapter, we'll take a look at the accessibility features that are part of Android. This is not an exhaustive guide; we'll focus on the features that may impact you as a developer, either because you need to provide support, make some decisions for the feature to work, or because it may change how your app looks or feels in some way. For a more consumer-focused introduction of features available, check Google's support pages.[1]

Android's accessibility features vary between device and vendor, as do many features on the platform. It's also possible to add third-party accessibility tools through the Google Play Store. A major aspect of accessibility is customizability. For users, the ability to pick a device with features that suit them, then add and customize those features as needed, is a boon. But this does mean your development target is a moving one, so manual testing across devices is essential. As a reference device for this chapter, I am using a Google Pixel running Android 10.

---

[1]https://support.google.com/accessibility/android

© Rob Whitaker 2020
R. Whitaker, *Developing Inclusive Mobile Apps*,
https://doi.org/10.1007/978-1-4842-5814-9_5

Features

Your device's accessibility settings are a top-level option in your system settings app. Android enables each option in this menu instantly when you toggle it. Most provide a short textual description of what the customization does and how. Many offer a visual example of the change you're making, and some even a tutorial. None of these settings are destructive, and you can disable them again by toggling off. So I'd recommend taking a few minutes to familiarize yourself with the content of these settings. Try enabling each one; in turn, navigate your app with the setting on, and see what differences it has made to your experience. Does your app still work as you would expect? Maybe you will discover some quick wins you can make from using your app with these accessible considerations enabled. Some of these settings, like TalkBack, change how you interact with your device. It's worth reading a little about these features first. But if you want to get stuck in, Android will give you a comprehensive tutorial the first time you toggle TalkBack. These accessibility settings are all about customizability, so you may find a setting that you want to enable on your own device.

Volume Key Shortcut

The volume key shortcut is an excellent tool for testing your app. It allows you to enable and disable a selected accessibility service quickly. Enable this service in your device's settings now. As we discuss different services, change which service this shortcut toggles in the service's settings. That way, you can get frustration-free access to the service wherever you are, without navigating to settings and back. Once enabled, press both of your device's volume keys for 3 seconds to toggle your chosen accessibility service.

The options available vary by device but include most of your device's installed accessibility services. We'll cover most of these features later in this chapter. For now, I'd suggest switching this to TalkBack. That way, you have a fast, easy way to enable TalkBack for accessibility testing. This should help to make screen reader device testing a regular part of your development flow.

TalkBack

When we talk about accessibility for mobile, we often are using the word accessibility as a proxy for screen reader navigation services like TalkBack. The chances are that if you know one Android accessibility service, it will be TalkBack.

Tip   Read the section on Navigating with TalkBack before enabling the service.

TalkBack is Android's built-in screen reader service. It enables blind and low-vision users to hear content available on the screen, but it is more than just a screen reader. By announcing controls and allowing users to interact with them through defined gestures, TalkBack allows your customers to navigate their entire device, without ever having to see the screen (Figure 5-1). Your app is already compatible with TalkBack, without requiring any setup on your part. But how well your app works with TalkBack is a different question. Android's in-built controls are all created with TalkBack in mind. So if you have used these controls as a base, you may find it works better than you might expect before you make any improvements.

Figure 5-1. *TalkBack highlighting the Display settings and reading the control's content*

TalkBack requires elements to have a textual representation so the element can be read to your customer. The information TalkBack reads and in what order varies by element. By default, TalkBack will read an element's text value if it has one. If your element's text is short, it may be missing context that visual users would derive from the elements around it. If your element's text is long, it may be too verbose for TalkBack users.

In these circumstances, a content description, a short descriptive string for accessibility, might work better. If present, Android TalkBack reads content descriptions instead of text values. TalkBack follows text or content descriptions with either a hint or a role where present; the order depends on the element's state and the type. We have covered these in more detail in the previous chapter. While TalkBack is just one accessibility service, it uses the same accessibility tree as any other. As a general rule, if your app works well with TalkBack, you'll find other accessibility services will work ok too.

For testing and learning purposes, I'd also recommend enabling the Display speech output setting. You can find this in TalkBack settings under Developer settings. This will show a toast with the current utterance on screen as it is being read. This should help you to understand precisely what you are presenting to your customer.

Android features a simple method of detecting a typical screen reader feature that may affect the functionality of your app. TalkBack allows users to interact with elements on the screen without activating them. This is done by tapping or performing touch gestures on the screen or on a specific element. This means these gestures are not passed through to your app and elements are activated differently. So it can be useful to know if your customer's device has this feature enabled as you may need to adjust how your app uses touch gestures as a result. You can do this by querying the isTouchExplorationEnabled property on Android's AccessibilityManager (Listing 5-1).

Listing 5-1. Determining if explore by touch is enabled

```
val a11yManager = getSystemService(Context.ACCESSIBILITY_SERVICE)
as AccessibilityManager
val isExploreByTouchEnabled = a11yManager.isTouchExplorationEnabled
```

For more on detecting if TalkBack or other accessibility services are enabled, see the section "Detecting Accessibility Services" later in this chapter.

Updating Content

Even with a perfect accessibility tree, you may find there are instances where you need to alert TalkBack users to a visual change on screen. This could be to inform your customer that a new message has arrived, a long running task has completed, or a score in a game has changed. There are two ways you can do this. But before you decide to add either feature, consider if you are adding value for your customer or merely adding noise.

Announce for Accessibility

At any time you can tell TalkBack to announce any string you pass with the announceForAccessibility() method (Listing 5-2). This method is available on any view.

Listing 5-2. Making TalkBack announce the screen has changed

```
myView.announceForAccessibility("New message received")
```

Live Regions

Live regions are areas of your screen where updated content appears separately to where a TalkBack user is interacting. An example could be a counter of the number of filtered search results displayed. While typing in a search field, a customer will want to know if greater or fewer results are being returned with each character they type, but navigating into and out of a search field with each letter would be laborious.

In these instances, you could mark your results counter as a live region (Listing 5-3 and Listing 5-4). A live region will announce its content each time it updates without any further interaction by your customer. There are two possible modes for live regions: `polite` and `assertive`. `polite` will read the content after any current utterances have finished. `assertive` will interrupt any existing announcements; avoid these unless absolutely necessary.

Listing 5-3. Creating a live region in XML

```
<TextView
    ...
    android:accessibilityLiveRegion="polite" />
```

Listing 5-4. Creating a live region in Kotlin

```
resultsCounter.accessibilityLiveRegion = View.ACCESSIBILITY_
LIVE_REGION_POLITE
```

NAVIGATING WITH TALKBACK

TalkBack changes the model of interacting with your app. Once you have enabled this service in your device's accessibility settings, TalkBack is running. So you must understand the changes it makes with how you interact with your device, not least so you can turn the feature off when you're finished!

TalkBack navigates all the readable elements of your screen's UI in natural direction – from top left to bottom right in most languages – highlighting each element with a bounding box as it progresses. You can select an element by tapping on it; a single tap will no longer activate controls. Swipe right anywhere on the screen to navigate to the next element or left for the previous. To activate a control, you must now double tap.

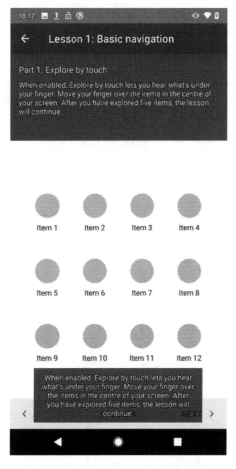

Figure 5-2. _Android's TalkBack tutorial app_

Fortunately, TalkBack features a fantastic tutorial app that allows you to practice using the screen reader's features. If this is the first time TalkBack has been activated on this device, TalkBack will launch it's tutorial as soon as you toggle the service on (Figure 5-2). If TalkBack has been enabled before, you can manually start this tutorial. Find it in the TalkBack settings toward the bottom of the list. To navigate there, remember – tap once to select an element; double tap to activate that element. Swipe right then left on a scroll view to page down. Complete the tutorial before trying anything else with TalkBack; it will save you a lot of frustration later.

Select to Speak

Select to Speak is a more "traditional" screen reader compared to TalkBack. Select to Speak will read any textual content that appears on the screen in the order it appears. Select to Speak doesn't provide any assistance with navigating or interacting with your app. This makes it an ideal tool for people who struggle to read because of low vision, dyslexia, or low literacy, for example.

Select to Speak has a few differences when compared to TalkBack regarding what it reads, how, and when. The intention for this tool is to assist with large amounts of text, an article, or eBook, for example, or more extensive passages of text. Select to Speak is not intended to assist with navigation or imply meaning from the layout. As such, Select to Speak reads content as it appears on the screen, ignoring any changes you have made to the accessibility tree. This includes ignoring grouped elements and content descriptions unless the element with the content description has no other text representation. For example, on the Google Play Store where TalkBack would read an app's rating as "four point two stars from 12 million reviews," Select to Speak will read "four point two. Twelve M reviews."

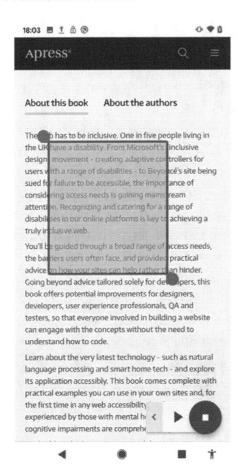

Figure 5-3. *Select to Speak enabled with an area being selected for reading*

Select to Speak adds an accessibility button to the bottom right of the screen. On tapping this, users have two options: press the Play button to read the whole visible screen in natural reading direction, or drag a finger over an area of the screen (Figure 5-3). This second option draws a bounding box; Select to Speak reads aloud any elements within the area of the bounding box.

Font Size

Android natively supports global scaling font sizes to fit your customer's preference (Figure 5-4). The number of options varies by vendor, but Google's Pixel devices support four settings, from small through to the largest.

Figure 5-4. *Android's smallest (left) and largest (right) font sizes. Appearance will vary by device*

You can achieve automatic font scaling in your app using scale-independent pixels; you'll see these in layout files as "sp" units (Listing 5-5). SP units represent pixels but with a few variable elements. This allows designers to specify a font size say 14px; we can then input this into XML as 14sp. At standard text sizes, this will then appear as the equivalent of 14px.

Listing 5-5. Setting text size by scale-independent pixels

```
<TextView
    ...
    android:textSize="14sp"
    android:layout_width="wrap_content"
    android:layout_height="wrap_content"  />
```

The variable elements to an sp unit are, firstly, screen density. 1sp at default text size on a screen with 160 dpi (dots per inch) is equivalent to 1 pixel. Screens with higher or lower dpi are scaled up or down appropriately. Whereas a fixed pixel figure would appear larger or smaller across different dpis, an sp unit should appear roughly the same. Secondly, sp units are scaled proportionally by the users chosen font size setting. This means ensuring all your text is set to SP units will maintain the appearance of your view while supporting accessibility.

A relevant consideration for adequately supporting the varying text sizes and screen densities of your users is the size you provide for elements displaying text. Avoid using fixed height or width dimensions providing wrap_content instead. Using and combining layouts like linear layouts and constraints layouts will allow text elements – EditText, Button, TextView, etc. – to grow and shrink as needed while maintaining your intended design. Any element that contains text should be presented inside a scroll view. This will ensure that users with any given combination of text size, screen size, screen density, etc. will still be able to read all of your content.

Display Size

Android's ability to support a vast range of screen shapes and sizes lends itself to frictionless support for another accessibility feature: adjustable display size (Figure 5-5). This works seamlessly for your app, providing you're following a few simple design guidelines: avoid fixed sizes for elements preferring `wrap_content`. Use flexible layouts such as constraints layouts. Place text content inside scroll views, and use relative instead of fixed units.

For example, a pixel will vary in physical size between screen resolutions, whereas millimeters will have a fixed size across devices but will take up proportionally different amounts of space on screen. Instead, it would be best if you defined all layout dimensions using sp units (scale-independent pixels) for text sizes and dp units (density-independent pixels) for non-text values (Listing 5-6). These values scale proportionally based on environment variables. These variables include your customer's settings for text size and display size, as well as their device's pixel density.

Listing 5-6. Defining a button's text size and padding using sp and dp units

```
<Button
    ...
    android:layout_width="wrap_content"
    android:layout_height="wrap_content"
    android:textSize="24sp"
    android:padding="16dp" />
```

Using sp and dp units will maintain your screen's layout across your users' myriad devices, as well as supporting scaled screen sizes and scaled text in a way that helps your customer while maintaining high standards of design.

Figure 5-5. *Android's smallest (left) and largest (right) display sizes. Appearance will vary by device*

Dark Theme

New for Android 10 is dark theme. I know many devs love to have interfaces with a dark theme. Because we spend hours looking at screens, it makes a massive difference to our eyes if we don't have white light shone at them. Plus, it does look pretty cool. But dark theming is also an important accessibility feature. Large amounts of bright light can be a problem for people with specific vision issues such as cataracts where light can cause discomfort and wash out the rest of the person's vision. The higher contrast on dark theming can also make it easier to distinguish between elements for people with reduced color perception or blurred vision. So while it's tempting to think of dark theming as nice to have, for many, it's an essential accessibility feature.

Supporting dark theme requires some changes to your app. Firstly, if you're not already, you'll need to compile against API level 29. The quickest way to support dark theme is to force your app to support dark mode by adding the line in Listing 5-7 to your app's theme in your styles. xml file.

Listing 5-7. Forcing dark theme support for an app style

```
<style name="AppTheme"
      parent="Theme.MaterialComponents.Light.DarkActionBar">
      ...
      <item name="android:forceDarkAllowed">true</item>
</style>
```

You may find this works for your app, but this is a pretty blunt instrument. We're using our original theme combined with Android's default dark theme behavior. We have no control here over exactly how our app works with the dark theme. The chances are we need to have some more fine-grained control over how things appear.

Android gives us the ability to define dark, or night, variations for each color we have defined in our palette. In Android Studio find the *res* directory in your project navigator. Right click, and select New ➤ Android Resource File. Name the file colors – it's ok that we already have a file with this name; we're making a night variant. Under Available Qualifiers find Night Mode (Figure 5-6), and press the Add button to select it. In the Night Mode dropdown box that has now appeared, change the value to "Night," and press OK.

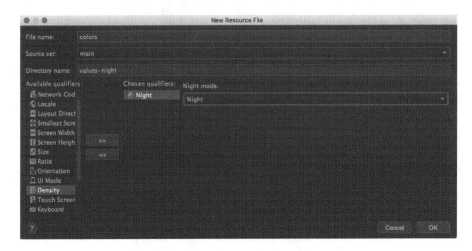

Figure 5-6. *Creating a night mode color file variant*

You'll then find you now have two color files appear in your project navigator. One with the suffix "*(night).*" (Figure 5-7)

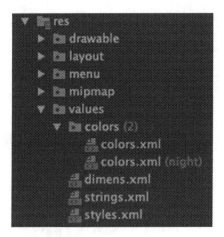

Figure 5-7. *Two color values XML files in Android Studio's project navigator. One as a night variant*

In this new night variant file, you can copy any color values from your original color values file that need dark theme variants. For example, if your standard background color is `<color name="background_color">#FFFFFF</color>`, you could add this to your night mode file as `<color name="background_color">#FF808080</color>`. This will make your background a dark gray color in dark mode, rather than Android's default black. Any colors you don't copy Android will adjust for you. For this to work, we need to ensure we're not using any hard-coded color values in any of our layout XML files or our app code. Always define colors in your colors.xml file, then refer to this defined color by name as in Listing 5-8 and Listing 5-9.

Listing 5-8. Referencing our background color value in a layout

```
<LinearLayout
    ...
    android:background="@color/background_color" >
```

Listing 5-9. Referencing our background color value in code

```
val color = getColor(R.color.background_color)
```

Magnification

Android features two magnification services. The magnified result is the same; the difference is how they are triggered. You can toggle magnify with triple tap, as the name suggests, by triple tapping anywhere on the screen. Magnify with shortcut (Figure 5-8) adds an accessibility shortcut button to the bottom right of the screen as part of the navigation bar. Tap the button once to toggle magnification on or off.

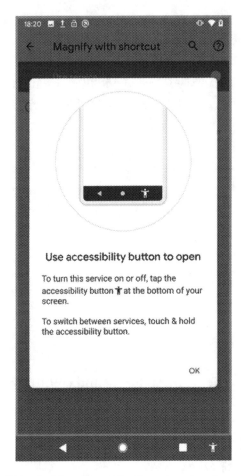

Figure 5-8. *Enabling Magnify with shortcut by the accessibility button*

Android developers need to be aware of magnification for two reasons, the first of which can affect any app. As text is written left to right, any magnification users will usually scan zoom down the left of your screen (or right in the case of right to left languages). This means if you have content that is not naturally (left) aligned, magnification users will often miss this. For example, if you add an icon conveying status next to a row in a table, if your icon is to the right of the text, a magnification user may not notice the status icon (Figure 5-9). Where possible, keep any meaningful content naturally aligned.

Figure 5-9. *Navigating accessibility settings with magnification enabled. Any right-aligned content may be missed*

Another feature of magnification that developers should be aware of is the gestures used. Triple-tap magnification will override any triple tap events that your app listens to, meaning if magnification is enabled, your app won't receive any triple tap gestures, even if your user hasn't activated the viewfinder. Once activated, magnification works using two finger swipes to move the viewfinder and two finger pinch gestures to zoom in and out. This means your app will not receive two finger swipe or pinch gestures once magnification is active. An ideal fix for this would be to modify the gestures your app uses once magnification is enabled or activated as appropriate. Unfortunately, as things stand, I haven't been able to find a way to detect if either of these magnification services is active. The method for detecting magnification services mentioned later in this chapter doesn't appear to return either of these services. This could mean a frustrating experience for magnification users who are expecting gestures to work in your app. This is just one reason why you should always provide alternatives to any touch gestures your app uses.

Color Correction

Color correction provides a selection of filters designed to assist users who experience color deficiencies. These filters help to increase contrast and shift colors away from those which deficiencies can cause problems differentiating. Android achieves this with a global overlay, so no work is required by developers to support color correction.

However, you should try out each of the filters available in your app to determine if contrast ratios with each filter are still high enough and to see if it's still possible to derive meaning from color use where needed. You should avoid using color as the only way to convey meaning, combining words and shapes too. An excellent example of this would be a status indicator; instead of a circle in either red or green, use a green circle and a red exclamation mark.

Color Inversion

Inverting colors has benefits for several impairments. It reduces glare and increases contrast. This means people with light sensitivity, color deficiencies, or reduced vision can all benefit from this feature. Color inversion inverts all colors on screen. This is regardless of where or how they are used and how your app is set up. This includes images and videos. Some users will benefit from inverted images, but for many, it will just look weird. A better experience for your customers, if possible, is to support dark theming. With dark theming, covered earlier, you can choose which colors your app inverts and how, resulting in a solid accessible experience, while maintaining a good-looking app.

Remove Animations

Animations can trigger vertigo and nausea in people with balance disorders. Animation can also be worrying and distracting for people with certain learning difficulties or disorders such as attention disorders, autism, and anxiety. For these reasons, it's necessary to listen to this setting and use it to determine if you should reduce or remove animation. With this setting enabled, you should look at places in your app where you have fast animation, animation in multiple plains, zooming animation, and auto-playing video.

There is no friendly Boolean value to determine if your user has enabled this setting, but the `ANIMATOR_DURATION_SCALE` setting will return a float value of 0 if this setting is on. So we can use the code in Listing 5-10 to turn this into a Boolean we can use in our code.

Listing 5-10. A method returning false if the user has requested animations removed

```
private fun areSystemAnimationsEnabled(): Boolean {
    val animationDuration = try {
        Settings.Global.getFloat(contentResolver,
    Settings.Global.ANIMATOR_DURATION_SCALE)
    }
    catch (e: Settings.SettingNotFoundException) {
        0f
    }

    return animationDuration != 0f
}
```

Switch Access

Switch access is an accessibility service intended to help people with limited motor abilities by allowing your user to navigate and control your interface using an external hardware device. A switch can be a number of things, for example, a regular keyboard. Third-party switches explicitly designed for this purpose are also available to purchase.

Tip   Read the section on Navigating with Switch Access before enabling the service.

Switch Access highlights each interactive element in turn with a bounding box. Your user can then press a switch to either skip to the next element or activate the current selected one. Navigating with one button is time-consuming, meaning Switch Access users are often the users most affected by any timeouts in your app. Consider extending or removing timeouts where possible.

Figure 5-10. *Switch Access highlighting a row of apps*

To achieve this control, the Switch Access accessibility service uses the accessibility tree discussed in Chapter 4. This is the same accessibility tree used by other services such as TalkBack. So if your app works well with TalkBack, the chances are it will be pretty good with Switch Access too. The difference compared to TalkBack is that Switch Access will only focus on interactive elements (Figure 5-10). For this reason, your interactive elements must be set up correctly. Use Android's built-in controls such as buttons and edit text controls, extending where needed rather than implementing your own. For example, if you use an image and add an onTouchListener, Switch Access won't access this touch listener. Instead, use an image button control.

NAVIGATING WITH SWITCH ACCESS

When enabling Switch Access for the first time, Android will present you with a setup guide (Figure 5-11). This app will take you through getting Switch Access configured, then give you a test area to get used to how Switch Access makes interacting with your device different.

Figure 5-11. *Switch Access setup guide*

To begin, connect a switch. While there are switches available specifically for Switch Access, I'd suggest for testing purposes a keyboard; either USB or Bluetooth is the best way to get started.

Select the control mode based on the number of switches you want to use (Figure 5-12). I'd suggest trying both of these modes out so you can get an idea of how your Switch Access users will experience your app.

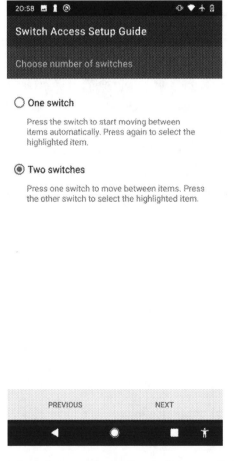

Figure 5-12. *Selecting the number of switches available to Switch Access*

Choosing One Switch, press your switch once to begin scanning the screen. The bounding box highlight will move automatically between interactive elements. Press the switch on an element to activate it. This form of interaction is prolonged but is essential for people with the most limited movement.

Two Switches is the more straightforward, faster mode of navigation as it is all done at the user's pace. One switch navigates to the next interactive element, the second switch activates that element. Select this option for now.

Next, choose your scanning mode (Figure 5-13). Linear scanning[2] highlights every interactive element in turn from top left to bottom right. This mode can be slower as we have to visit every element on screen but it does guard against some accidental presses. Row–column scanning will group elements by row. This makes navigating some screens faster. Pressing the "Next" switch will navigate to the next row of elements, rather than the next element. If you want to activate an element in that row, press the Select switch. Then use the "Next" switch to navigate to the element in that row that you want to activate.

---

[2]Android does warn that Linear Scanning mode doesn't work with keyboards, although I have never found this to be the case.

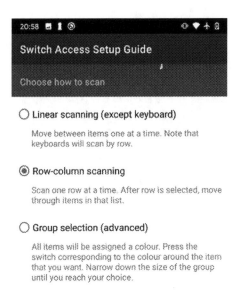

Figure 5-13. *Choosing a scanning mode in Switch Access Setup*

The next two screens cover choosing your two switches. Pick any two keys on your keyboard, but I'd suggest two that are close to each other.

Finally, we're presented with a game of tic-tac-toe to help us practice (Figure 5-14). Press your assigned "Next" key to begin scanning. If you're stuck with navigating with this setup or want to try something different, press Previous (the screen still works with regular touch input) and reconfigure. Before you disable Switch Access, remember to navigate your app with it too.

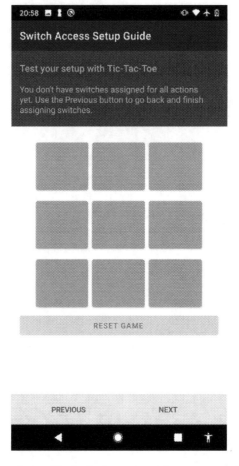

Figure 5-14. *Practicing Switch Access with a game of tic-tac-toe*

If you're feeling adventurous, try out some of the other options available in the Switch Access settings. They all make a noticeable difference in how the interface of your app is presented to your user. I'd recommend checking out the following:

- Auto-scan

  When Switch Access is configured with one button, auto-scan will automatically navigate from one element to the next in second intervals.

- Point scan

  A horizontal line scans from the top of the screen to the bottom;
  press Select to stop (Figure 5-15). A vertical line then moves
  from left to right. Press Select when the crosshairs are over the
  element you want to activate.

Figure 5-15. *Switch Access in Point Scan mode selecting the Drive app*

- Speech, sound, and vibration
  Enable spoken feedback in this menu. This mode combines
  the features of TalkBack with Switch Access by reading
  all text-representable elements aloud. This means switch
  control will focus on all elements while navigating, not only
  interactive ones.

Touch and Hold Delay

Touch and hold delay adjusts the time required for a long-press event to be fired. This helps to control for accidental presses. If you are determining long presses using an onLongClickListener this setting will be taken into account for you. Use this listener rather than attempting to time a long click yourself.

Time to Take Action

Time to Take Action, or the Accessibility Timeout as its also known, gives users extra time to see temporary visual elements and take action on them if needed. Accessibility users are often slower to navigate apps than non-accessibility users. Sometimes this is because of their abilities; others, it's a function of their chosen assistive technology.

This feature provides various options from 10 seconds to 2 minutes. Any subsequent toasts or snack bars will be displayed for the users-chosen length of time, overriding the value you have set in code. If you have implemented your own snack bar-type control, you won't get this behavior.

Captions

Android natively supports captions with the VideoView control. Users can enable these globally in the accessibility settings, as well as choosing options such as size and color (Figure 5-16). As a developer, you can either embed captions into the video track or provide them separately via an input stream in the vtt format – vtt subtitle tracks usually end with a .srt extension (Listing 5-11). Once you have done this, VideoView will handle rendering these as per your user's preference.

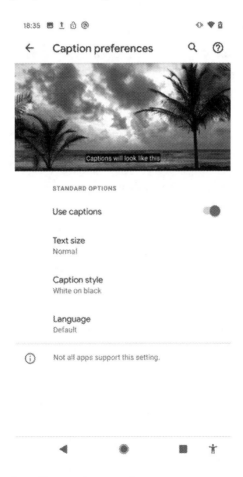

Figure 5-16. *Android's caption preferences*

Listing 5-11. Loading a subtitles file from resources and adding these subtitles to a VideoView instance

```
val subtitlesEN = getResources().openRawResource(R.raw.subs_en_vtt)
// this could also be an InputStream instance loaded from a network
   resource.
```

```
videoView.addSubtitleSource(subtitlesEN,
      MediaFormat.createSubtitleFormat("text/vtt",
      Locale.ENGLISH.getLanguage()))
```

If you're displaying video in a control other than the VideoView, you are responsible for displaying and rendering the captions yourself. You can retrieve your customer's settings using the CaptioningManager class seen in Listing 5-12.

Listing 5-12. Accessing caption settings from the system's captioning manager

```
val captioningManager = getSystemService(Context.CAPTIONING_
SERVICE) as CaptioningManager
val captionsEnabled = captioningManager.isEnabled
val captionStyle = captioningManager.userStyle
val textScale = captioningManager.fontScale
```

The CaptioningManager class provides a userStyle value returning a CaptionStyle class object as seen above. This class provides information such as the font, foreground and background colors, and more. Check the Android developer documentation for the full range of values.[3] You should follow these preferences as much as possible, as your customer will have chosen this combination of font, size, color, etc. for a reason.

---

[3]https://developer.android.com/reference/kotlin/android/view/
accessibility/CaptioningManager.CaptionStyle.html

Additionally, you should listen to changes in your customer's caption settings. CaptioningManager allows us to set a CaptioningChangeListener (Listing 5-13) so we can be notified our customer changes a setting.

Listing 5-13. Using a CaptioningChangeListener to detect changes in captioning settings

```
class MyCaptionListener:
    CaptioningManager.CaptioningChangeListener() {
    override fun onEnabledChanged(enabled: Boolean) {
            // remove captions from your view
    }
}

class MainActivity : AppCompatActivity() {
    override fun onCreate(savedInstanceState: Bundle?) {
        super.onCreate(savedInstanceState)
        val captioningManager = getSystemService(Context.
        CAPTIONING_SERVICE) as

        captioningManager.addCaptioningChangeListener(MyCaption
        Listener())
    }
}
```

High-Contrast Text

High-contrast text makes text either black or white, depending on the text's original color. A border of the opposite color is then added (Figure 5-17). This is done using Android's regular text rendering system, so it will be processed for you in most instances. AccessibilityManager does have a value to detect if this feature is enabled. But, for unclear reasons, this is hidden from the public interface. So if you chose to access the isHighTextContrastEnabled method, do so with care.

Figure 5-17. *Standard text (left) and high-contrast text (right)*

Voice Access

Voice Access is not included as part of Android's standard accessibility suite but is an accessibility service downloadable for free from the Google Play Store by searching for Voice Access. Voice Access allows completely hands-free access and control of the device. This is a helpful feature say if you're driving, but it's invaluable for people with limited mobility, especially those with the most limited movement but who can speak. Voice Access uses voice alone not just to perform simple tasks such as the Google Assistant but to fully control the device. As well as being a significant accessibility feature, Voice Access is really fun to use, so download it from Google Play and check it out.

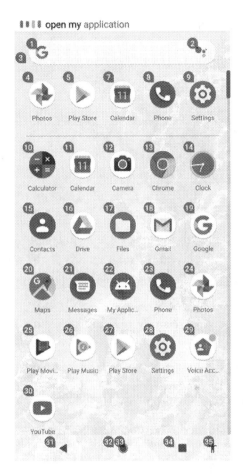

Figure 5-18.   *Voice Access enabled. User has requested "Open my*
application"

Like other accessibility services on Android, Voice Access uses the
accessibility tree we discussed in Chapter 4. For simplicity, Voice Control
will display numbers next to every interactive element (Figure 5-18), but
these can also be triggered by the name displayed on the screen. Whereas
TalkBack will read an element's content description over the element's
text value, Voice Access will respond to the element's text value, but not
the content description as this is not visible. As with Switch Access, if you

127

add a tap or click listener to an element that is not usually a control, say an image, for example, Voice Access will not recognize this as an element that can be interacted with. Stick with Android's standard controls whenever possible; in this instance, always use an ImageButton.

Localization

Android's localization support is comprehensive and well developed, to the point where it's probably simpler to build an app ready for localization than one that isn't. Android Lint will also remind you if you ever do code something that isn't ready for localization. While your app may only be available in one territory, creating an app ready for localization is good practice regardless. It will save you a lot of effort in future when you want to make changes to strings or other resources. Plus, the option for localization opens your business up to new markets. Even in a single market, you'll find more people than you might anticipate who would prefer your app to be available to them in another language. The US Census Bureau found that nearly 22% of Americans, around 70 million people, spoke a language other than English when at home.[4]

When creating a new app, Android Studio will create a strings.xml file for you (Listing 5-14). As a good practice, always add any strings used in your user interface here. Give your string a name value; this is what you will use in code to reference your string, then add your string between the <string> tags. While this section deals with localized strings, you can localize any other resource in the same way, including layouts, drawables, dimensions, and others.

---

[4]"New American Community Survey Statistics for Income, Poverty and Health Insurance Available for States and Local Areas," United States Census Bureau, September 14, 2017. https://www.census.gov/newsroom/press-releases/2017/acs-single-year.html.

Listing 5-14. A strings.xml file as generated by Android Studio

```
<resources>
    <string name="app_name">My Application</string>
    <string name="action_settings">Settings</string>
</resources>
```

To use these string resources in your app, refer to them by the name you provided in the string value. Consider our `action_settings` string . We can refer to this in a layout XML file using `@string/action_settings` (Listing 5-15) or in code using `R.string.action_settings` (Listing 5-16).

Listing 5-15. Accessing a string resource in a layout xml file

```
<item
    ...
    android:title="@string/action_settings" />
```

Listing 5-16. Accessing a string resource in code

```
val string = getString(R.string.action_settings)
```

Translating Your App

Don't be tempted to use an automated service to generate translations. These services don't understand the context of your app and can often result in meaningless and confusing messages for your customers. Google provides a translation service through the Google Play Developer Console. While translations will vary by app size and by your choice of language, Google suggests the price is usually around $50US per translation per app.

Before we send our app for translation, spend some time annotating the contents of your existing strings.xml file. Add comments above strings explaining where the string is used and what its purpose is. Include any restrictions or requirements you have for that string. This will help your translator pick the most appropriate word or phrase for each usage.

To create a localized version of your strings, choose File ➤ New ➤ Values Resource File. Call the file strings to match the original and select the Locale modifier in the list on the left (Figure 5-19). Press the Add button. A new list appears of Android supported locales. Select the locale you want to localize for – you can type in this list to filter it – and press OK. You'll see you now have two strings.xml files in the project navigator, your original and your newly localized one (Figure 5-20).

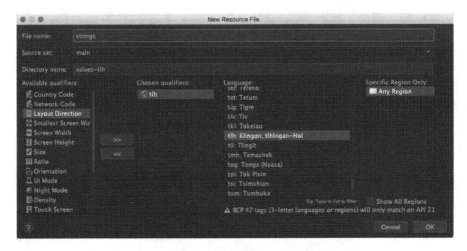

Figure 5-19.   *Creating a new localized strings.xml file*

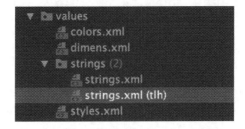

Figure 5-20.   *Two strings files in our project navigator, one as a "tlh" localized variant*

In your new strings file, copy any of the XML string entries that need translating, and change the value between the `<string>` tags to your newly translated value. Any string you chose not to localize here will fall back to your original strings.xml file's value.

Keyboard Navigation

Android supports full navigation through a keyboard or remote control (Figure 5-21). In fact, certain Android apps, such as ones made for Android TV, require this functionality. Connect a USB or Bluetooth keyboard to your phone, and as well as typing, you can use tab or arrow keys to navigate between elements. Android will use your app's accessibility tree to determine the order to present elements but will sometimes need some hints. So it's worth connecting a keyboard to find out if your screen navigates as you'd expect.

Figure 5-21. *Keyboard Navigation with Drive selected*

Detecting Accessibility Services

Android's AccessibilityManager (Listing 5-17) service will provide you with a range of information about the accessibility environment for the device on which your app is running.

Listing 5-17. Getting the accessibility service

```
val a11yManager = getSystemService(Context.ACCESSIBILITY_SERVICE)
as AccessibilityManager
```

We can discover more about the accessibility services available, what is currently running, and what these services can provide for our customer by querying this manager. To get a list of all installed accessibility services, we can request installedAccessibilityServiceList (Listing 5-18).

Listing 5-18. Getting a list of all currently installed accessibility services

```
val a11yManager = getSystemService(Context.ACCESSIBILITY_SERVICE)
as AccessibilityManager

val installedServices = a11yManager.installedAccessibility
ServiceList
```

Running Services

While the list of installed services will tell us what your customer's device is capable of, it doesn't mean any of these services are in use. The accessibility manager provides a Boolean value telling us if one or more services are currently running (Listing 5-19).

Listing 5-19. Detecting an accessibility service. Returns true if any service is running

```
val a11yManager = getSystemService(Context.ACCESSIBILITY_SERVICE)
as AccessibilityManager

val isAccessibilityEnabled = a11yManager.isEnabled
```

Now we know an accessibility service is running, we might want to dig a little deeper into what type of services are running. To see if we need to make changes, we need to know what the service's capabilities are. We can do this by querying the Accessibility Manager. There is no direct request to detect if TalkBack is enabled, for example, as your customer may be using a screen reader from their handset vendor or a third-party screen reader from the Google Play Store. Instead, we query based on the service's capabilities. Android then returns us a list of all running services with that feature. For a list of currently enabled accessibility services, we can use the `AccessibilityManager`'s `getEnabledAccessibilityServiceList` method (Listing 5-20). We need to pass a constant representing the type of service we want to know about.

Listing 5-20. Getting a list of all running screen readers

```
val a11yManager = getSystemService(Context.ACCESSIBILITY_SERVICE)
as AccessibilityManager

val screenReaders = a11yManager.getEnabledAccessibilityService
List(AccessibilityServiceInfo.FEEDBACK_SPOKEN)
```

The `FEEDBACK_SPOKEN` constant passed as the argument to this method returns any service that is capable of providing spoken word feedback such as TalkBack. We can pass different constants to this method to return different types of service as required. These constants are divided by the type of feedback the service provides to your user or the capabilities the accessibility service has. To return any services that can provide any kind of feedback, pass `AccessibilityServiceInfo.FEEDBACK_ALL_MASK`. To return any running service regardless of capability or feedback type, pass `AccessibilityServiceInfo.DEFAULT`. We'll cover all the constant values here.

Feedback

These constants characterize how services provide feedback to your user. Fetching services by the type of feedback they can provide means the service is currently running. It doesn't necessarily mean that feedback type is presently enabled or active. Services can fall into multiple feedback types.

- FEEDBACK_ALL_MASK

  All services that provide any type of accessibility feedback to your customer.

- FEEDBACK_AUDIBLE

  Services that provide auditory, but not spoken, feedback.

- FEEDBACK_SPOKEN

  Spoken word services such as TalkBack.

- FEEDBACK_BRAILLE

  Braille services.

- FEEDBACK_GENERIC

  A catch-all property for services that don't fit into other feedback categories.

- FEEDBACK_HAPTIC

  Services providing haptic feedback.

- FEEDBACK_VISUAL

  Visual services such as overlays, color filters, etc.

Capabilities

These constants allow us to request accessibility services grouped by their abilities. Fetching services by their ability doesn't necessarily mean this capability is currently enabled or active. Services can fall into multiple capability categories.

- `CAPABILITY_CAN_CONTROL_MAGNIFICATION`

  An accessibility service that can control screen zoom levels.

- `CAPABILITY_CAN_PERFORM_GESTURES`

  A service that has the ability to mimic touch gestures on the device's screen.

- `CAPABILITY_CAN_REQUEST_FILTER_KEY_EVENTS`

  Any service that can request to filter the events received by your app from keys. This includes device hardware keys such as a camera button but also from connected devices such as keyboards and game pads.

- `CAPABILITY_CAN_REQUEST_FINGERPRINT_GESTURES`

  Accessibility services that can capture events and gestures from the device's fingerprint sensor.

- `CAPABILITY_CAN_REQUEST_TOUCH_EXPLORATION`

  Accessibility services, such as TalkBack, that allow users to explore UI elements by tapping on them without necessarily activating them. This feature can also prevent certain touch gestures from being passed to your app if running.

- `CAPABILITY_CAN_RETRIEVE_WINDOW_CONTENT`

  These services can access the content of your app when presented in the current active window.

- `DEFAULT`

  The default value if no other capability is presented by the service. Passing this will return any running services.

Summary

- Android accessibility features vary by device and vendor. Extra accessibility services can be downloaded from the Google Play Store.

- Always use Android's provided UI elements, extending them where needed. Avoid creating your own controls as its almost impossible to match the accessibility features of the standard controls.

- Listen to your customer's preferences, and respect them; failure to do this can cause angry customers.

- Try out the accessibility features available on your device; what's the worst that could happen? You might find something that benefits you.

This chapter gave us an overview of the accessibility features and services available on Android phones. We also covered ways we developers can support them better, ways the features might affect our apps, and how we can detect and respond to our customer's preferences. In the next chapter, we'll move onto iOS, and start looking at how the iOS accessibility system works.

CHAPTER 6

iOS Accessibility Model

Before we dig into the accessibility features available, it's useful to know a little about how Apple's accessibility features work on a low level. We're all familiar with the visual user interface presented by our app. It's what you see and interact with on our device's screen. Our visual user interface is made up of the controls, text, and images we add in code or through Interface Builder. These are pulled together with stacks or constraints and finished with some appropriate color. But your app has a second user interface, the Accessibility User Interface, or accessibility tree.

Accessibility Tree

When your UIKit screen appears, iOS builds an accessibility tree of elements on the screen in natural reading order (top left to bottom right in most languages). This creates an Accessibility User Interface (AUI) as Apple refer to it, for your user's chosen assistive technology.

Because of the declarative nature of SwiftUI, iOS doesn't have to infer our intention from a visual representation. Instead, iOS builds the AUI from SwiftUI code by removing any layout-only elements.

© Rob Whitaker 2020
R. Whitaker, *Developing Inclusive Mobile Apps*,
https://doi.org/10.1007/978-1-4842-5814-9_6

Each Accessibility Element on the AUI includes the following information about the elements available: label, value, hint, traits, and actions; we'll cover each of these in this chapter. The AUI doesn't create accessibility tree nodes for layout-only elements such as stack views. But iOS does use them to help decide the order elements should appear in the accessibility tree.

Accessibility Protocol and Accessibility Attachment Modifier

The Accessibility Protocol is implemented by all of Apple's provided UIKit elements. This protocol is responsible for handing the accessible metadata about each element. Apple has set sensible default values for each view. This means any custom subclass you create should only require tweaking, rather than full implementation of this protocol.

SwiftUI's Accessibility Attachment Modifier contains equivalents for most of UIKit's Accessibility Protocol properties. To avoid duplication, I have covered both here.

Accessibility Element

iOS creates the Accessibility User Interface from any elements in your view that are marked as accessible and ignores any elements marked as not accessible. Apple has set some sensible defaults for the controls they provide. Views that are accessible by default include UILabel, UITextField, UIProgressView, and any view that extends UIControl. Other views, such as UIImageView and UIView itself, are not accessible by default.

At times, it may be appropriate to make non-accessible elements available to assistive technology (for example, see the discussion on Alternative Text for Images in Chapter 3) or vice versa, disabling views that would typically be accessible (see the section "Semantic Views" later in this chapter for more on this). Having too many, or inappropriate, views marked as accessible creates noise for assistive technology users. Having too few means these users lose context and functionality.

To customize which elements are accessible, each UIKit element has an isAccessibleElement property (Listing 6-1). This can be set to true or false as required in code. Interface Builder features a corresponding checkbox under the Accessibility heading in the Identity Inspector (Figure 6-1). SwiftUI elements can be set to accessible or otherwise by adding the modifier .accessibility(hidden:) to your view with a Boolean value (Listing 6-2).

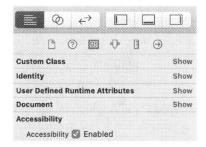

Figure 6-1. *Accessibility Element checkbox in Interface Builder*

Listing 6-1. Setting a view hidden to accessibility in UIKit

```
detailLabel.isAccessibleElement = false
```

Listing 6-2. Setting a view visible to accessibility in SwiftUI

```
Image(systemName: "heart.fill")
    .accessibility(hidden: false)
```

Caution   If you are creating a custom control or view with interactivity, avoid subclassing UIView. UIControl is usually a better option as this class is already set up with sensible accessibility defaults. If you do choose to subclass UIView, be sure to test this thoroughly with accessibility users.

Label

An element's Accessibility Label is the first string read by VoiceOver when an accessible element receives focus. It should be used to quickly identify what that element is or does, not necessarily what the content of that element is. Think of this as your element's name. By default, most views already have an accessibility label. This is your element's text value. You might need to add an accessibility label if your view has no text value, such as a button with an image, or if your label is very long.

Ideally, labels should convey the meaning in one word, such as "Play" or "Like," for example. Your labels should be capitalized, and don't end them with a period. Don't include the type of element as this is redundant and will add noise.

An element's accessibility label can be set in Interface Builder under the Identity Inspector tab. Or you can set it in code with the `accessibilityLabel` property (Listing 6-3). In SwiftUI, this can be set using `.accessibility(label: "Send")` (Listing 6-4).

Listing 6-3. Setting an accessibility label in UIKit

```
playButton.accessibilityLabel = "Play"
```

Listing 6-4. Setting an accessibility label in SwiftUI

```
Image(systemName: "heart.fill")
    .onTapGesture { ... }
    .accessibility(label: "Like")
```

Value

The accessibility value is the current value of the element. This could be text entered in a text field, the current numerical value of a slider, or the current status of a switch, for example. Typically, your accessibility value will be defined for you by your control. For example, a UISlider subclass will always set the accessibility value to the current slider value.

There are times when you will need to set this value yourself. If you're creating a custom view subclass, you will need to determine which data you consider the value. If you group subviews together into a semantic view with various values, you will need to make a decision on which value to present or in what order. If multiple elements have values, a semantic view might not be the best option.

You can set this using the accessibilityValue property in UIKit (Listing 6-5). In SwiftUI the .accessibility(value:) modifier can be applied (Listing 6-6). Both take a string as an argument.

Listing 6-5. Setting an accessibility value in UIKit

```
playButton.accessibilityValue = "100"
```

Listing 6-6. Setting an accessibility value in SwiftUI

```
Image(systemName: "heart.fill")
    .accessibility(value: "100")
```

When using VoiceOver, adding a value to a control reads the same as adding the value to the end of the label. As such, I've commonly seen values added to labels. While this works fine for VoiceOver, this will have a negative effect for Braille keyboard and Voice Control users. Braille keyboards display values in a separate register, indicating they are adjustable. Voice Control will listen to element labels. Adding a value onto the end of this requires greater accuracy from your customer.

Hint

VoiceOver reads an element's Accessibility Hint last, after a short pause. Use the hint to give further context around what the result of performing this element's action is, but only if this consequence is not immediately evident from the element's Accessibility Label. VoiceOver users can disable

143

hints and often just skip them. For this reason, it's best to assume your customer won't hear them. Use hints as a fallback to provide additional information, never something crucial to your UI.

In their guidance on writing good Accessibility Hints,[1] Apple suggests you imagine describing the controls action to a friend. For example, you might say "tapping the send button sends your message." Providing your accessibility traits and label have been correctly set up, it is redundant to inform your user the name of the element, the type of control, and the action it performs. So, if we strip these out, your hint would be "Sends your message." Avoid "send your message" as this sounds like an instruction, rather than guidance. Hints should begin with a capital letter and end with a period.

An elements accessibility hint is a string property that can be set in Interface Builder under the Identity Inspector tab (Figure 6-2). It can be configured in code with the `accessibilityHint` property (Listing 6-7). In SwiftUI, this can be set using `.accessibility(hint: "Sends your message.")` (Listing 6-8).

Figure 6-2. *Setting an accessibility hint and label in Interface Builder*

---

[1]`https://developer.apple.com/library/archive/documentation/`
`UserExperience/Conceptual/iPhoneAccessibility/Making_Application_`
`Accessible/Making_Application_Accessible.html#//apple_ref/doc/uid/`
`TP40008785-CH102-SW6`

Listing 6-7. Setting an accessibility hint in UIKit

```
sendButton.accessibilityHint = "Sends your message."
```

Listing 6-8. Setting an accessibility hint in SwiftUI

```
Button("Send") { ... }
    .accessibility(hint: "Sends your message.").
```

Traits

Accessibility traits are fundamental to how iOS builds an accessibility model. Accessibility traits are available on any UIView subclass. Apple has done a fantastic job setting defaults on every view and control they provide. This means, for the most part, you won't ever have to change what Apple has provided. But that doesn't mean it isn't worth your time checking whether these default traits are logical. Apple doesn't know precisely how you're using the elements you've picked. Also, traits can vary as the status of a control changes. For example, if you create a stopwatch app, the time label will update every second, or millisecond, when the stopwatch is running. Here it would make sense to use the trait updatesFrequently. Say the user presses the Lap button, and we freeze this time and add a new row into a UITableView where the time continues. The original label has now frozen the time and won't change. Marking this label as updatesFrequently no longer makes sense. Instead we should set the identifier to staticText.

Accessibility traits can be set in Interface Builder (Figure 6-3) by checking (or unchecking) a box next to the trait you want to change. In code, these can be set using the accessibilityTraits property on any UIView (Listings 6-9 to 6-14). accessibilityTraits is a bitmask to enable it to hold multiple traits simultaneously.

Listing 6-9. Setting a single trait removing all others in UIKit

```
accessibilityTraits = .none
```

Listing 6-10. Adding a trait to existing traits in UIKit

```
accessibilityTraits.insert(.button)
```

Listing 6-11. Removing a single trait in UIKit

```
accessibilityTraits.remove(.selected)
```

Listing 6-12. Adding a single accessibility trait in SwiftUI

```
.accessibility(addTraits: .isHeader)
```

Listing 6-13. Adding multiple accessibility traits in SwiftUI

```
.accessibility(addTraits: [.isHeader, . updatesFrequently])
```

Listing 6-14. Removing accessibility traits in SwiftUI; multiple traits can be removed with an array as above

```
.accessibility(removeTraits: .playsSound)
```

Figure 6-3. *Setting accessibility traits in Interface Builder*

Traits vary slightly in name and availability across UIKit, SwiftUI, and Interface Builder (Table 6-1). We'll cover each trait in turn and what effect this has.

Table 6-1. *Accessibility trait names*

Interface Builder	UIKit	SwiftUI
Button	.button	.isButton
Image	.image	.isImage
Static Text	.staticText	.isStaticText

(continued)

147

Table 6-1. (*continued*)

Interface Builder	UIKit	SwiftUI
Search Field	.searchField	.isSearchField
Plays Sound	.playsSound	.playsSound
Keyboard Key	.keyboardKey	.isKeyboardKey
Summary Element	.summaryElement	.isSummaryElement
User Interaction Enabled	.notEnabled (inverse of IB checkbox)	No direct trait, but inferred from a control's .enabled() constructor
Updates Frequently	.updatesFrequently	.updatesFrequently
Starts Media Session	.startsMediaSession	.startsMediaSession
Adjustable	.adjustable	--
Allows Direct Interaction	.allowsDirect Interaction	.allowsDirect Interaction
Causes Page Turn	.causesPageTurn	.causesPageTurn
Header	.header	.isHeader
Link	.link	.isLink
Selected	.selected	.isSelected
--	--	.isModal
--	.tabBar	--
(all checkboxes deselected)	.none	--

None

This element has no particular accessibility traits.

Button

This element is an interactive button. This trait causes VoiceOver to announce "button" after reading the text of the item. It also makes the element visible to Voice Control and Switch Control.

Link

An in-line link such as in a web page that navigates to a different screen. This trait causes VoiceOver to announce "link" after reading the item's text. This trait tells Voice Control and Switch Control this element is interactive.

Search Field

A text field that allows your customer to enter a string to search. This trait differentiates this field from a standard text field. It hints to the user that entering text here should cause the UI to update elsewhere.

Image

Any image or visual element that has no text and no actions, that is, you shouldn't apply this trait to an image button. See the discussion on Alternative Text for Images in Chapter 3 for guidance on when to make images accessible.

Selected

An item that is currently selected, such as a tab, or item on a segmented control.

Plays Sound

An element that will trigger sound once activated. This tells VoiceOver to stop any utterances when this element is activated.

Keyboard Key

An item that acts as a key on a keyboard, for example, if you are implementing a custom input control. This allows direct interaction with the key, as well as VoiceOver focus.

Static Text

Text that does not change throughout the life cycle of your view.

Summary Element

A Summary Element trait characterizes an area which provides an overview of the information on the screen. The best example of this is Apple's built-in Weather app (Figure 6-4). On opening a location, VoiceOver focuses on the top area which is marked as a Summary Element. VoiceOver then reads a summary of the current weather conditions in the selected location.

Figure 6-4. *Apple's Weather app with VoiceOver highlighting the top*
Summary Element

Not Enabled

This item is disabled, and nothing will happen if activated. Note that
Interface Builder presents this checkbox as the inverse, User Interaction
Enabled. In SwiftUI, there is no direct equivalent of this trait. SwiftUI
determines as this property from the view's `.disabled()` constructor.

Updates Frequently

This trait is for elements that update either their label or value too frequently to post a `UIAccessibilityLayoutChangedNotification` notification. This tells your user's chosen assistive technology to poll this element for value and label changes at suitable intervals. An example use case for this would be a time display.

Starts Media Session

Used for an element that starts playing or recording media once activated. This trait causes VoiceOver speech to be paused once the element is activated, preventing the media session being interrupted.

Adjustable

Use this trait for elements such as sliders or pickers, where the user can choose from a range of values. Make sure your control also implements `accessibilityIncrement()` and `accessibilityDecrement()`. We'll cover these later in the chapter. This trait has no corresponding trait in SwiftUI.

Allows Direct Interaction

Allows Direct Interaction tells VoiceOver there should be no deviation from the standard UIKit touch control for this view.

Imagine you have created a music app that provides a piano keyboard for the user to play (Figure 6-5). Using the VoiceOver paradigm of swiping to key and double tapping would not produce much of a tune. Allows Direct Interaction disables VoiceOver gesture navigation for this control only. This allows your user to play the keyboard by tapping the keys without disabling VoiceOver for the rest of the UI. Inappropriate use of this trait will create a worse experience for your VoiceOver users.

Figure 6-5. *Apple's Garage Band app with VoiceOver highlighting the keyboard view. This view has the trait Allows Direct Interaction. Allowing multi-touch interaction on the keyboard while maintaining VoiceOver navigation of the controls above the keyboard*

Causes Page Turn

This trait indicates to screen readers that this content represents one page out of a set of pages, such as an eBook.

This trait causes a screen reader to call the `accessibilityScroll()` method on this view immediately after completing reading the content. The screen reader will then begin to read any new content. Reading will stop if the content does not change after calling this function.

Header

The title of a navigation bar or any large text header element that divides content.

By swiping vertically, or by adjusting the rotor control, VoiceOver users can leverage this trait to skim your content. This helps determine which content is relevant to their needs without having to scan the whole screen.

Tab Bar

This trait indicates a view that is not directly interactive but contains tab buttons that can be interacted with. Any element with this trait must return false for `isAccessibilityElement`.

Modal

This trait is only available in SwiftUI. It is the SwiftUI version of UIKit's `accessibilityViewIsModal` property. This trait causes assistive technologies to ignore the contents of any other views on screen and allow access only to the children of this view.

Language

An element's Accessibility Language property allows us to specify the language rules we want VoiceOver to use for this element (Listing 6-15). It is a string value following the BCP 47 specification[2] that tells VoiceOver it should read this element's accessibility label, value, and hint in a language other than the user's system language. If no alternative language is required, there is no need to set this value.

Listing 6-15. Setting an element's accessibility language

```
// es-419 is the code for Latin American Spanish.
spanishGreeting.accessibilityLanguage = "es-419".
```

---

[2]www.rfc-editor.org/rfc/bcp/bcp47.txt

Elements Hidden

Elements Hidden, `accessibilityElementsHidden` (Listing 6-16), is a UIKit only Boolean value. It tells assistive technology any child views are not accessible. You might use this where a view is partially obscured by another view which has animated over.

Listing 6-16. Setting children of contentView hidden to accessibility

```
contentView.accessibilityElementsHidden = true
```

View Is Modal

`accessibilityViewIsModal` (Listing 6-17) is a UIKit-only Boolean property. It causes assistive technologies to ignore any views on the screen outside this one. Assistive technologies can then access only the children of the view where this is set. In SwiftUI, you can do the same by applying the `.isModal` trait.

Listing 6-17. Setting the customAlert view modal for assistive technologies in UIKit

```
customAlert.accessibilityViewIsModal = true
```

Element Order

Assistive technologies present the screen from top left to bottom right. Most of the time, this is correct for our interfaces. But sometimes this makes reading the screen illogical. This can happen if you have staggered elements in your interface or if you are presenting elements vertically.

Take the App Store as an example. On the listings page for an app or game, just under the app's icon is a bar with some details about the app: a star rating with the number of ratings beneath, a ranking with the app category beneath, and an age rating with the heading "age" beneath. If VoiceOver were to read this without any modifications to our AUI, the result would be "4 stars. Number 1. 12+. 14K ratings. Strategy. Age." This information is jumbled and meaningless.

Instead, it would make more sense for VoiceOver to read "4 stars. 14K ratings." To do this, our subviews can tell accessibility if it's elements should be accessed in a specific order. Each subview we create returns an accessibilityElements array to UIAccessibility. iOS will typically generate this for us, but we can have a little more control. In this example (Listing 6-18), we're using a UIView subclass as a container for three header and three detail elements. We have an @IBOutlet reference to each element; then we're telling UIAccessibility the order we'd like these elements to be traversed. Any element we don't add to this array will be ignored by assistive technology.

Listing 6-18. Informing UIAccessibility of the order we'd like our elements traversed in a subview

```
class DetailView: UIView {

    @IBOutlet weak var header1: UILabel!
    @IBOutlet weak var header2: UILabel!
    @IBOutlet weak var header3: UILabel!
    @IBOutlet weak var detail1: UILabel!
    @IBOutlet weak var detail2: UILabel!
    @IBOutlet weak var detail3: UILabel!

    override var accessibilityElements: [Any]? {
        set{}
        get{
            return [header1!,
                    detail1!,
                    header2!,
```

```
            detail2!,
            header3!,
            detail3!]
        }
    }
}
```

Escape

Navigating with an assistive technology is often slower than without for several reasons. Sometimes too, context can be lost that might be clearer when viewing the screen as a whole. For this reason, Apple provides some global shortcuts. One of these is the Magic Tap; we cover this in the section on VoiceOver later in the book. Another shortcut that works with VoiceOver, but also Switch Control, is Escape (Listing 6-19).

Figure 6-6. *Switch Control's Escape command*

With Switch Control, the Escape option is available from the actions menu when any element is selected (Figure 6-6). When using VoiceOver, an escape can be performed by drawing a Z shape on the screen with two fingers. If you're using a standard UINavigationController, you receive this behavior for free. Where you may find you need to use this is if you're presenting custom modal elements.

Listing 6-19. Supporting the accessibility Escape command

```
override func accessibilityPerformEscape() -> Bool {
    // Dismiss the current view.

    return true // return false if the view can't be
dismissed.
}
```

Custom Actions

One great way to speed up accessibility navigation, and create a far better experience for accessibility users, is to use custom accessibility actions. Custom actions allow us to add actions to elements that can only be accessed through assistive technologies. In Switch Control, these actions are displayed in the control options when the control is focused (Figure 6-7). With VoiceOver, the control will read "actions available" when the element is selected. The actions can then be cycled by swiping vertically.

Figure 6-7. *A custom accessibility action for "10 Travelers"*

To determine any custom actions available, the accessibility API will query your view's `accessibilityCustomActions` property (Listing 6-20). This returns an array of any actions available. Create new actions by initializing a `UIAccessibilityCustomAction` object. Your action should return true if it was successful.

Listing 6-20. Returning a new custom accessibility action for a view subclass

```
override var accessibilityCustomActions:
[UIAccessibilityCustomAction]? {
    set {}
    get {
        return [UIAccessibilityCustomAction(name: "10
        travelers") { customAction in
            self.slider.value = 10
                return true
        }]
    }
}
```

Control Focus

In some situations, it can be useful to know when an element receives or loses focus through an assistive technology, say if you need to change the status of a view or want to add an assistive highlight. The accessibility API provides two functions for you to receive updates for these events. `accessibilityElementDidBecomeFocused()` and `accessibilityElementDidLoseFocus()` (Listing 6-21). These events are triggered by both VoiceOver and Switch Control.

Listing 6-21. Listening for changes in accessibility focus for an element

```
override func accessibilityElementDidBecomeFocused() {
    // this element became focused, change status as needed.
}

override func accessibilityElementDidLoseFocus() {
    // this element lost focused, reset the elements status.
}
```

Frame and Activation Point

accessibilityFrame (Listing 6-22) marks the bounds that assistive technologies like Switch Control will use to draw the highlight when focusing on an element. This will usually be the frame of your view, but if you do need to extend the frame, this property allows you to do this.

Listing 6-22. Setting a custom accessibility frame

```
myView.accessibilityFrame = CGRect(x: myView.frame.origin.x - 10,
    y: myView.frame.origin.y - 10,
    width: myView.frame.size.width + 20,
    height: myView.frame.size.height + 20)
```

If you do adjust your element's frame, you should also set the activation point. This is the point on the screen that assistive technologies will synthesize a tap when activating the control. You can do this by passing a CGPoint to accessibilityActivationPoint.

Increment and Decrement

Some assistive technologies change how we interact with elements on the screen. VoiceOver and Switch Control are two examples; we'll cover more of how and why they do this in later chapters. But this means we need a new paradigm for controls that require more than a simple tap for activation. Sliders are a great example of this. UIKit's UISlider control implements two functions, accessibilityIncrement() and accessibilityDecrement().

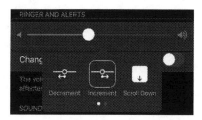

Figure 6-8. *Switch Control's Increment and Decrement controls*

Any views that use the .adjustable accessibility trait must override these two functions. The functions will be called by your user's assistive technology when they perform an increment or decrement action. This can be tapping an increment switch on Switch Control (Figure 6-8) or swiping vertically with VoiceOver. There is an issue with how iOS presents UISlider controls to accessibility, however, so let's take a look at fixing this. You should do something similar in your own apps whenever using a UISlider control. This will also give you the knowledge to create your own accessible adjustable controls if you choose to do this. In general, I would always recommend using UIKit's provided controls.

ACCESSIBLE SLIDER

Clone the git repo for this book, and under Chapter 6, look for the slider exercise. Here we'll create an accessible slider control.

This example is a section of an app that allows customers to book vacations to different parts of our solar system. The screen included in this example is the detail for the listing for the planet Mars. In the center of the screen, we have a slider control to let our customer input how many travelers they are booking for. When you increment or decrement the slider, we update the label above to show the number chosen.

If you try this control out with VoiceOver, here's what's read. "Travelers: 0." Then we swipe to the slider. "zero percent, adjustable." If we then perform the accessibility increment action by swiping up with VoiceOver, the reply is "10 percent."

There are a few issues here for accessibility that we can fix. While space is a dangerous place, I don't envisage any of our customers wanting to take a percentage of a traveler with them, instead they will prefer whole people. So we should change VoiceOver's response. Also, how would a blind user know what the purpose of this slider is? There is a label before of "Travelers," but how do we know this slider controls that value?

We can fix both of these issues by grouping the two elements together. In this example, I've already put both elements inside a UIView subclass. The subclass handles the label updates when the slider is changed. In your own project, add your slider and label into a view if you haven't already done this.

First, we need to tell the accessibility API a little information about our container view. It needs to know the view is accessible and that it is adjustable. Let's do this in the init.

```
required init?(coder: NSCoder) {
    super.init(coder: coder)

    isAccessibilityElement = true
    accessibilityTraits.update(with: .adjustable)
}
```

Now if you run VoiceOver on this screen, your container view will be focused, and you'll be told its adjustable. But there is no label, and nothing happens if we try to adjust it. So right now we've just made the experience worse. Let's add an accessibility label and value.

```
override var accessibilityLabel: String? {
    set{}
    get{
        return "Travelers"
    }
}

override var accessibilityValue: String? {
    set{}
    get{
        return "\(Int(slider.value))"
    }
}
```

Now accessibility users can know what the control is for, but they still have no way to control it. This is where we use the accessibilityIncrement() and accessibilityDecrement() functions. In this example, we just want our slider to change, and the code we've already written will handle the rest. So all we need to do is to pass these interactions through to the slider. If you're creating your own custom control, you'll need to add appropriate logic here to handle each interaction.

```
override func accessibilityDecrement() {
    slider.accessibilityDecrement()
}

override func accessibilityIncrement() {
    slider.accessibilityIncrement()
}
```

There's one more behavior we need to update. With the original slider, VoiceOver would announce to us the percentage value of the slider each time we changed it. This wasn't that helpful for us as the values of slider controls are floats, so VoiceOver always read us a percentage value. But that behavior was much better than what we hear now, which is nothing at all. So let's mimic this behavior, but make it a little more appropriate for our use. We are already updating the visual label in our code in the sliderValueChanged() function. This feels like the best opportunity to update VoiceOver customers too. Find this function, and we have one line to add after our existing code.

```
@IBAction
func sliderValueChanged() {

    ...

    UIAccessibility.post(notification: .announcement,
        argument: "\(rounded)")
}
```

Now when we run VoiceOver on this control, we have fewer swipes and added clarity. Using accessibility tools together in this way to create compound accessibility views is a technique known as semantic views. It is a powerful tool, and essential if you want to make the most accessible interfaces possible.

Semantic Views

Creating semantic views are a must if you want to take your app's accessibility to the next level. A semantic view is a view made of multiple elements, grouped together for accessibility because they have meaning, or a semantic, together. This technique is about pulling together all accessible user interface tools we have covered in this chapter. The aim is to make an interface that is simpler to understand and faster to navigate for accessibility customers.

You'll notice semantic views used regularly throughout iOS when you navigate using an assistive technology. Take a look at the table cell in Figure 6-9 from iOS' Files app. There are several pieces of information here: the file name, date, size, and a button to download. If these were presented individually, that would be four swipes with VoiceOver. And it wouldn't be clear which file would be downloaded if we activated the download button. Instead, you can see VoiceOver has highlighted the cell as one element.

Figure 6-9. *VoiceOver highlighting a cell and its content as one semantic view*

Sometimes iOS can be smart enough to create semantic views for you on some `UITableViewCell` designs. Most of the time, we will need to create them manually. There are several ways to build semantic views.

Custom View

We covered this technique in the Accessible Slider exercise earlier. In that exercise, we used a UIView as a container. We created a custom UIView subclass for view. This view then handled the accessibility interactions and fed information back to the accessibility API on behalf of our control. This is my preferred method because this component is then reusable across your app. iOS also gives you a lot for free using the standard UIAccessibility and UIView functions.

Frame

Another way of creating semantic views is to adjust a view's accessibilityFrame to encompass other elements. You can then remove the overlapped elements from the accessibility tree by setting isAccessibleElement to false. Pass any other element's accessibility properties as needed to the view with the expanded frame.

This technique requires you to calculate frames carefully and recalculate them if your layout changes. Say your customer changes their font size or rotates the screen, for example. Using this method is best for simple views, likely ones without any interaction. If the view you're expanding is a control, you need to set the accessibilityActivationPoint to ensure assistive technologies activate your control, not the center of your expanded frame.

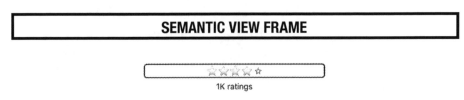

Figure 6-10. *Accessing these two labels separately with VoiceOver is unnecessarily verbose*

An example of where you might use this technique is for elements you have stacked vertically. If we want to display a star rating with the number of reviews beneath, it makes sense for us to group these as one element. First, let's add a couple of lines into our `viewDidLoad` callback to set up the label and hide the unneeded view from accessibility.

```
class ViewController: UIViewController {

@IBOutlet weak var rating: UIButton!
@IBOutlet weak var responses: UILabel!

override func viewDidLoad() {
    super.viewDidLoad()

    responses.isAccessibilityElement = false
    rating.accessibilityLabel = "\(stars) stars from \
    (respondents) ratings"
    }
}
```

The second step is to calculate the frame. We need to do this in `viewDidLayoutSubviews` to ensure iOS recalculates the accessibility frame if the view changes.

```
override func viewDidLayoutSubviews() {
    super.viewDidLayoutSubviews()

    let ratingX = Float(rating.frame.offsetBy(dx: 0,
dy: 0).origin.x)
    let responsesX = Float(responses.frame.offsetBy(dx: 0,
dy: 0).origin.x)

    // Find the left-most item.
    let x = CGFloat(fmin(ratingX,
                                responsesX))
    let y = rating.frame.origin.y
```

```
    let ratingWidth = Float(rating.frame.offsetBy(dx: 0,
dy: 0).size.width)
    let responsesWidth = Float(responses.frame.offsetBy(dx: 0,
dy: 0).size.width)

    // Match the width of the widest element.
    let width = CGFloat(fmax(ratingWidth,
                                    responsesWidth))

    // Calculate the height of both elements plus the padding
between each.
    let height = rating.frame.size.height + padding + responses.
frame.size.height

    rating.accessibilityFrame = CGRect(x: x,
                                        y: y,
                                        width: width,
                                        height: height)
}
```

Figure 6-11. *Our new semantic view uses just one swipe and is more meaningful*

If the element that is now acting as your semantic view is a button, one more step is needed. Remember to tell assistive technologies that the accessibilityActivationPoint is over the button element, not in the center of the frame. Do this in viewDidLayoutSubviews so it is calculated each time your screen changes.

```
override func viewDidLayoutSubviews() {
    super.viewDidLayoutSubviews()

    ...
```

```
rating.accessibilityActivationPoint = CGPoint(x: rating.
frame.midX,
     y: rating.frame.midY)
}
```

SwiftUI Stacks

One of the compelling accessibility changes in SwiftUI is a mechanism to create semantic views with a single modifier. In SwiftUI much of your layout is done using stacks, either an HStack, VStack, or ZStack. Each of these stacks can contain many views of different kinds. The standard behavior is for the stack to presents all these views to accessibility in the order they appear in the stack. Using the .accessibilityElement(childr en:) modifier, we can change this behavior.

If we pass .combine to the accessibilityElement modifier, assistive technologies don't focus on each of the elements individually. Instead, they focus on the stack, and each of the stack's children's accessibility properties is passed to the stack.

Often you can give your customers a better experience using the .ignore value. Ignore, predictably, ignores all of the views inside the stack. Ignore also makes the stack focusable. But stacks have no accessibility properties of their own, so we need to add any labels, traits, hints, and actions. If we wanted to make a view similar to the preceding rating view, our code would look like Listing 6-23.

Listing 6-23. SwiftUI semantic view

```
VStack (alignment: .leading, spacing: 10) {

    Button("☆☆☆☆") { self.tappedRatings() }
        .font(.largeTitle)
```

```
    Text("1K ratings")
        .font(.subheadline)
}
.padding()
.accessibilityElement(children: .ignore)
.accessibility(label: Text("\(stars) stars from \(respondents)
ratings"))
.accessibility(addTraits: .isButton)
.accessibilityAction { self.tappedRatings() }
```

Twitter Example

Twitter provides an excellent case study for where semantic views make a huge difference. Try navigating the iOS Twitter app with both Switch Control and then VoiceOver enabled, and note the experience when reading a tweet. Try out some other Twitter clients if you have them, and see how each does this differently.

When you're visually browsing a timeline, you're not checking out avatars, Twitter names, handles, tweets, links, likes, retweets, and more. You're looking at tweets. But each tweet is made up of a whole bunch of other things. Here's a tweet from Accessibility London meetup (Figure 6-12); VoiceOver is highlighting the tweet. If VoiceOver focused on every element, this would make navigating Twitter really frustrating. Let's take a look at how we might create something similar.

Figure 6-12. *A tweet focused by VoiceOver*

SEMANTIC CELL

From the GitHub repo for this book, open the Semantic Cell example. Here we have a custom table cell for a social media post. We have the user's avatar, name, and post contents. Underneath we have the number of comments, likes, and shares. Each of these is a button to let us comment, like, or share. The avatar is also a button to the user's profile.

Startup VoiceOver and see what is read for this cell. iOS has already done a lot of work for us by grouping all the cell's contents together. Swipe to the next element, and you'll be presented with one of the buttons on this post, not the next post in the timeline. This will make navigating hundreds of posts very time-consuming.

First, let's remove the username from the accessibility label. This isn't really relevant and adds noise for VoiceOver users. We do this by setting our own accessibility label.

```
class SemanticCell: UITableViewCell {

    ...

    var model: TimelineEntry! {
        didSet{
            ...
```

```
            accessibilityLabel = "\(model.user.name). \(model.
            content)"
        }
    }
}
```

Next, we should remove the buttons from the accessibility interface. This will mean smoother navigation between posts.

```
class SemanticCell: UITableViewCell {

    ...

    var model: TimelineEntry! {
        didSet{

            ...

                comment.isAccessibilityElement = false
                share.isAccessibilityElement = false
                like.isAccessibilityElement = false
                avatar.isAccessibilityElement = false

        }
    }
}
```

Great, except that now our accessibility users can't access these functions. Let's add them back as accessibility actions. For the purpose of this exercise, we won't actually add any code in the actions. In your own app, you'll want to add some code here.

```
class SemanticCell: UITableViewCell {

    ...

    var model: TimelineEntry! {
        didSet{

            ...
```

```
            let likeAction = UIAccessibilityCustomAction(nam
e: "Like, \(model.likes)") {_ in
                return true
            }
            let shareAction = UIAccessibilityCustomAction(name:
            "Share, \(model.shares)") {_ in
                return true
            }
            let commentAction = UIAccessibilityCustomAction(name
            : "Comment, \(model.comments)") {_ in
                return true
            }
            let profileAction = UIAccessibilityCustomAction(name
            : "view \(model.user.name) profile") {_ in
                return true
            }
            accessibilityCustomActions = [commentAction,
            likeAction, shareAction, profileAction]
        }
    }
}
```

Summary

- The system that controls how assistive technologies interact with your app is shared across all iOS' assistive technologies.

- Apple calls this the accessible user interface; you may be familiar with the same concept called the accessibility tree.

- iOS does a lot for us out of the box; stick with standard iOS controls for your views, and your app's accessibility will be okay. Test your app, ideally with real accessibility users, to find out where you need to make tweaks.

- Semantic views are an essential technique to take your app's accessibility to the next level.

Now that you know how iOS accessibility works under the hood; let's cover some of the accessibility tools iOS has available for your customers. We'll find out how you can best support them and what considerations you might need to make if you find your customer has enabled one of these features.

CHAPTER 7

iOS Accessibility Features – General

Apple's Human Interface Guidelines[1] (often known as the HIG) are essential reading for anyone creating mobile apps for iOS – not just designers. The HIG sets out how Apple has worked to make UIKit flexible for you as an app developer but also clear and meaningful to your users.

The section on Accessibility[2] is the starting point when considering how to introduce accessibility to your iOS app. The HIG gives you the best overview of using iOS' built-in accessibility considerations. Keeping your apps consistent with this guide (not just the accessibility section) will help your users feel at home within your app, as many of the system patterns designed by Apple will carry over into your app and others. Plus, following this guide and ensuring a high level of accessibility mean your app is much more likely to get featured on the App Store. Both UIKit and SwiftUI provide powerful customization options to allow you to maintain accessibility while giving your app a distinctive look and feel.

---

[1] https://developer.apple.com/design/human-interface-guidelines/
[2] https://developer.apple.com/design/human-interface-guidelines/
 accessibility/overview/introduction/

© Rob Whitaker 2020
R. Whitaker, *Developing Inclusive Mobile Apps*,
https://doi.org/10.1007/978-1-4842-5814-9_7

People use Apple's accessibility features, such as reduced transparency, VoiceOver, and increased text size, to personalize how they interact with their devices in ways that work for them. An accessible app supports such personalization by design and gives everyone a great user experience, regardless of their capabilities or how they use their devices.

—Apple Human Interface Guidelines: Accessibility

I asked Apple's Accessibility team about the feedback they receive from their customers regarding the accessibility of third-party apps. They told me:

The two most common bits of feedback that we receive about the accessibility of third-party apps involve element labels and the order of navigation for VoiceOver. Additionally, color palette choices, Dark Mode support, and media captioning are all great practices.

—Apple Accessibility Team[3]

We cover accessibility labels in the section "Accessibility Protocol" of Chapter 6. Later in that chapter, we also include techniques for improving navigation order such as semantic views. For accessibility rules on choosing colors, see the Distinguishable guideline in Chapter 3. For guidance on including captions, see Chapter 10.

In this chapter, we'll cover iOS system-wide accessibility features, why someone may enable them, and how having them enabled might affect your app. This is not an exhaustive list of accessibility settings; for more details on what's available from an end-user perspective, see the

---

[3]Email to the author.

accessibility section of Apple's web site.[4] Instead, this chapter focuses on accessibility settings that might change the way your app looks or works or settings that might require you to add code or make decisions to best support them.

In UIKit if you're using the recommended system APIs – Dynamic Type, Accessibility Traits, etc., you'll get many of these features for free. SwiftUI's accessibility support is far better than UIKit, for reasons covered in the previous chapter, but will still require some customization. If you're creating a non-native app through web views, or another cross-platform system, accessibility tools will often ape those of the system you're compiling for. Ultimately as with anything cross-platform, features will vary and may be limited. While Apple will do as much as possible for you, some settings will require you to query iOS' `UIAccessibility` framework for settings and make your own decisions about how to handle them.

From iOS 13 onward, the Accessibility menu is now a top-level menu in the system settings (Figure 7-1), grouped under four headings covering the class of impairment the technology is aimed to help with – general, vision, hearing, and physical and motor. iOS 12 and earlier, these features are found in the devices system settings, under General ➤ Accessibility.

---

[4]`www.apple.com/uk/accessibility`

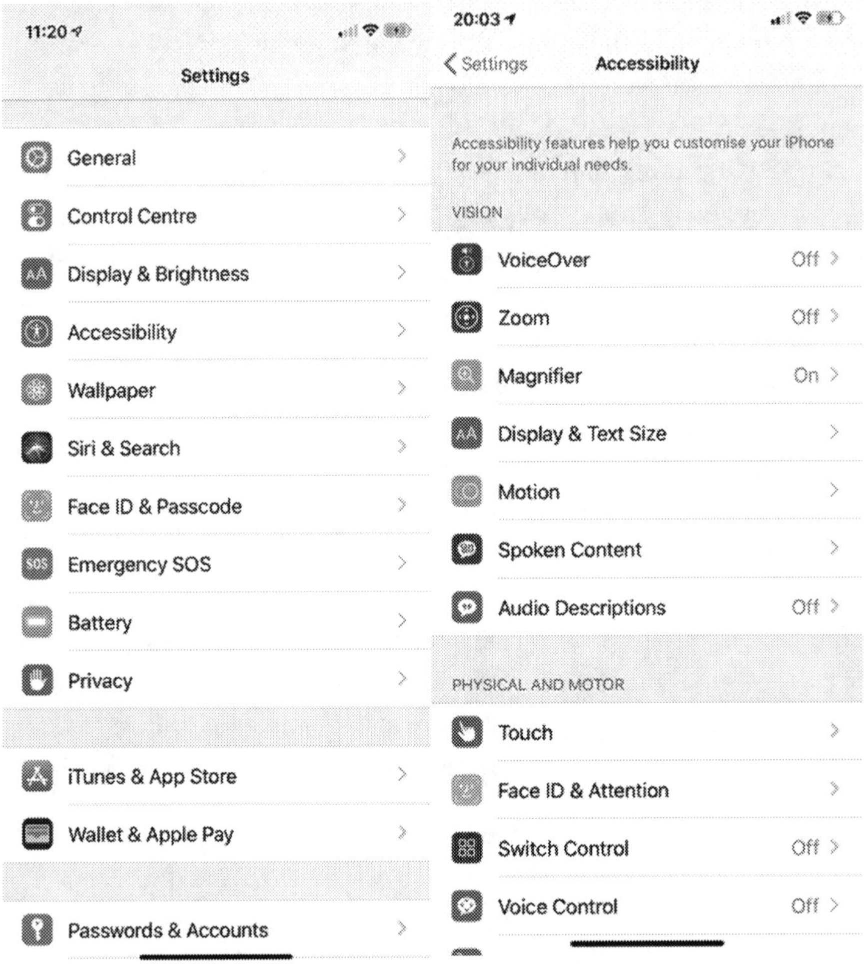

Figure 7-1. *Accessibility settings in iOS 13 (right) found in the top level of device settings (left)*

Each accessibility option in this menu provides a short description of what enabling this option does. Each option is instantly enabled and present system-wide once triggered. Guided Access requires an additional step to activate the feature once enabled.

Take some time to go through this menu; enabling each one, navigate through your app, and see how each option changes how your app looks and behaves. No setting is destructive and can be instantly disabled. Some settings, however, such as VoiceOver, do change how your device functions. So it's worth reading a little about the features first, at least so you know how to disable them when you're done. This menu is all about customizability, so you may find options you want to keep enabled on your personal device.

General Features

Apple breaks down its accessibility considerations into four categories – cognitive, motor, vision, and hearing (Figure 7-2). For this reason, I have broken the accessibility settings into four similar categories. Motor, vision, and hearing mirror Apple's categories. While there aren't specific settings to benefit those with cognitive impairments, many other settings will also help those falling into this category. In this first section, we'll cover some of the general settings and features of iOS.

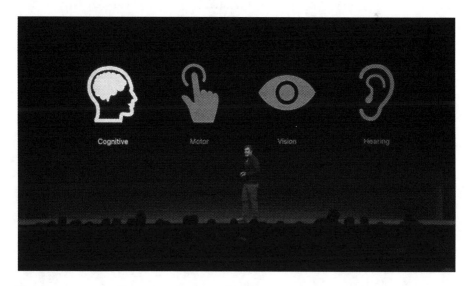

Figure 7-2. *Apple presenting its four categories of accessibility considerations at WWDC 2018*

Accessibility Shortcut

I mention this first, as this will allow you a quick and easy way to enable many accessibility features on iOS. Therefore, it is the best way to test your apps work with many iOS accessibility tools. Having this simple feature enabled will encourage you to activate these features as a regular part of your development and testing workflows. Importantly, it's also the simplest way to disable these features, which can save a lot of frustration once you've enabled a feature that changes how your device works.

Tip   Enable the Accessibility Shortcut before trying out anything else in this chapter.

Enable the accessibility shortcut in the accessibility settings on your device by going to Settings ➤ Accessibility ➤ Accessibility Shortcut. You'll find Accessibility Shortcut as the last item on the list. I highly recommend enabling every item on the list, so you can try these out quickly when needed.

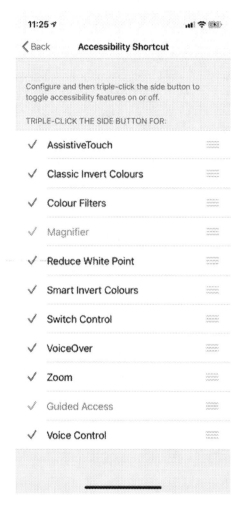

Figure 7-3. *Enable every option available in this list for easy access to that feature later*

The options available on this menu are Assistive Touch, Classic Invert Colors, Smart Invert Colors, Color Filters, Magnifier, Reduce White Point, Switch Control, VoiceOver, Zoom, Guided Access, and Voice Control (Figure 7-3). However, the exact options may vary depending on the settings for your device. I recommend enabling each one of these on your testing devices; we'll cover most of these features in more detail in this chapter.

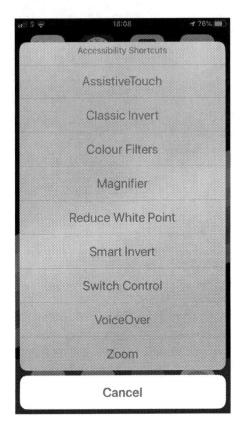

Figure 7-4. *Accessibility shortcut activated after pressing the home or sleep button three times*

You can then activate the accessibility shortcut when required by triple tapping the side button or home button on older devices. This presents a modal menu (Figure 7-4) where you can activate or deactivate the features you chose from the preceding list. I highly recommend keeping this shortcut enabled, as it doesn't affect your regular use of the iPhone but gives you pain-free access to accessibility tools when you want to check something out.

Control Center

A second quick access way of toggling accessibility features, albeit a rather more limited one, is through Control Center. Swiping down from the top of the screen, or bottom-up on a device with a home button, will show a bunch of buttons providing quick access to common device controls (Figure 7-5). The controls displayed are customizable through your device's Settings app. Follow Control Centre ➤ Customize Controls. Accessibility controls available here are Dark Mode, Guided Access, and Text Size. There is also an option to toggle the Accessibility Shortcut with the same options we chose in the setting we looked at above. Users with paired hearing aids can control them here too.

Figure 7-5. *Control Center with accessibility controls on the bottom row. L–R Text Size, Accessibility Shortcut, Dark Mode, and Guided Access*

Guided Access

Guided Access allows a device to be locked only to the current app and disable certain app and system features. Guided Access makes the device into a stand-alone kiosk device and is often used in retail settings where you might not wish to give the public unrestricted access to a device. Guided Access is primarily designed, however, to be helpful for people with a range of different needs: Those with learning difficulties can easily get confused by new things or not fully understand the consequences of specific actions. People with motor issues can sometimes cause accidental input and are then unable to return the device to a state they can use. People who suffer from anxiety of attention-deficit disorders can become overwhelmed by too much stimulus. In all of these situations, restricting the options available is desirable.

Guided Access needs to be enabled in the device's accessibility settings. Once enabled, it can be activated by using the accessibility shortcut of pressing the side or home button three times (Figure 7-6). Guided access is enabled per-app session and must be disabled to exit the app.

Figure 7-6. *Setting up Guided Access*

You can detect if Guided Access is activated by checking
isGuidedAccessEnabled and receive updates from
guidedAccessStatusDidChangeNotification (Listing 7-1) when this
setting is changed. In your app, you can use the status of this setting to
decide whether to lock down individual features, such as settings, or
destructive actions.

Listing 7-1. Registering for notifications in guided access status

```
import UIKit

class MyViewController: UIViewController {

    var guidedAccessStatus: Bool {
        get{
            return UIAccessibility.isGuidedAccessEnabled
        }
    }

    override func viewDidLoad() {
        super.viewDidLoad()

        NotificationCenter.default.addObserver(self, selector:
        #selector(guidedAccessChanged), name: UIAccessibility.
        guidedAccessStatusDidChangeNotification, object: nil)
    }

    @objc
    func guidedAccessChanged() {
      // check guidedAccessStatus for current status.
      // Hide features as appropriate.
    }
}
```

A better way to leverage this is to implement the
UIGuidedAccessRestrictionDelegate on startup of your app. This
delegate allows you to set custom actions that can be enabled or disabled
on request when a customer enables guided access within your app. For
example, you might add restrictions for "Settings" or "Delete Items." This
could then be configured by the person setting up guided access to enable
the guided access user to customize settings to their preferences but not
allow them to delete any items.

First, we need to create unique strings for each feature our users might want to disable. Creating these as an enum (Listing 7-2) allows us to keep this type safe and provide the additional data we need.

Listing 7-2. Providing unique strings for Guided Access features

```
enum Restriction: String, CaseIterable {
    case settings = "com.myCompany.myApp.restriction.settings"
    case delete = "com.myCompany.myApp.restriction.delete"
}
```

Next, we need human-readable strings for iOS to display to our customer – a short string used as a button label, then a longer descriptive string. Let's extend our enum in Listing 7-3 to associate those values with the unique string.

Listing 7-3. Associating human-readable strings with our restrictions enum

```
extension Restriction {
    var title: String {
        switch self {
        case .settings:
            return "Settings"
        case .delete:
            return "Delete"
        }
    }

    var detail: String {
        switch self {
        case .settings:
            return "Allow changing settings"
```

```
    case .delete:
        return "Allow permanent deletion of items"
    }
  }
}
```

Now we need to provide these strings to iOS in our app delegate by conforming to the UIGuidedAccessRestrictionDelegate (Listing 7-4). There are two protocol methods and one variable we need to conform to. The guidedAccessRestrictionIdentifiers variable is an array of unique strings for iOS and our app to identify features by. Then we have two functions, textForGuidedAccessRestriction and detailTextForGuidedAccessRestriction, where we provide our human-readable strings. To keep things neater in our app delegate, let's do this in an extension.

Listing 7-4. Providing our Guided Access strings to iOS

```
extension AppDelegate: UIGuidedAccessRestrictionDelegate {
    var guidedAccessRestrictionIdentifiers: [String]? {
        return Restriction.allCases.map { $0.rawValue }
    }

    func textForGuidedAccessRestriction(withIdentifier
    restrictionIdentifier: String) -> String? {
        return Restriction(rawValue: restrictionIdentifier)?.title
    }

    func detailTextForGuidedAccessRestriction(withIdentifier
    restrictionIdentifier: String) -> String? {
        return Restriction(rawValue: restrictionIdentifier)?.
        detail
    }
}
```

Finally, we need to handle iOS' callbacks when our user changes the Guided Access status of a feature (Listing 7-5). For this we need to conform to another delegate function in our extension, guidedAccessRestriction(with Identifier restrictionIdentifier: didChange:). This function provides us with a newRestrictionState enum value of either .allow or .deny.

Listing 7-5. Handling user changes in Guided Access feature status

```
    extension AppDelegate: UIGuidedAccessRestrictionDelegate {

...

func guidedAccessRestriction(withIdentifier
restrictionIdentifier: String,
didChange newRestrictionState: UIAccessibility.
GuidedAccessRestrictionState) {

        switch restrictionIdentifier {
        case Restriction.settings.rawValue:
            if newRestrictionState == .deny {
                // remove settings feature
            } else {
                // add settings feature
            }

        case Restriction.delete.rawValue:
            if newRestrictionState == .deny {
                // remove delete feature
            } else {
                // add delete feature
            }
```

```
    default:
        preconditionFailure()
    }
  }
}
```

Additionally, your app can query the guidedAccessRestrictionState (forIdentifier: String) function on the UIAccessibility API at any time to determine the status of a restriction (Listing 7-6). This can then be used to decide whether to deny an action or perhaps, preferably, hide an option altogether.

Listing 7-6. Detecting the current status of a Guided Access restriction

```
import UIKit

class MyViewController: UIViewController {

    override func viewDidLoad() {
        super.viewDidLoad()

        let deleteFeatureState = UIAccessibility.guidedAccess
        RestrictionState(forIdentifier: Restriction.delete.
        rawValue)

        switch deleteFeatureState {
        case .allow:
            // enable the delete feature
        case .deny:
            // disable the delete feature
        @unknown default:
            preconditionFailure()
        }
    }
}
```

Localization

Localization is built throughout iOS. While translating your app into different languages can be complex and nuanced, the coding to support this is not. You may feel your app doesn't need localizing as your business is currently only available in one country, but this doesn't reflect our global society. A significant number of people in any market will not have the market's primary language as their first. Plus, removing hard-coded strings from your code is general good code health.

You'll likely find your app is set up to begin localization even if you haven't localized anything yet. But to check, go to your project's settings, and scroll to the bottom (Figure 7-7). Here you'll find a section for localizations. Ensure "Use Base Internationalization" is checked, and you're good to go.

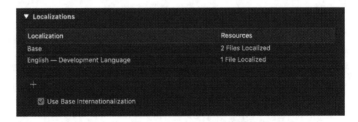

Figure 7-7. *Xcode Project's Localization settings*

From here you can press the + button to add a new language localization and begin the process of getting your app translated. To send your app's strings to a translator, go to Xcode's Editor menu, and choose Export for localizations. This will create all the files a translator will require. When you get your translation back, visit the same menu and select Import Localizations. Before you do this, however, there are a few changes you'll need to make to your app.

Views

Any xib or storyboard file can be localized, and this means more than just strings.

Using autolayout is essential with localization, as it is with dynamic type. It is not possible to guarantee the visual length of your string will be for each localization. Many languages take up much more space than English. English's 12-character localization becomes the 13-character Lokalisierung in German, while in simplified Chinese, it's the 3-character 本土化. You can test this using pseudolanguage; we'll cover this in Chapter 11.

Consider too that some languages, Arabic, for example, are written right to left. iOS will do a great job of flipping your UI for you, but this is based on autolayout constraints. So failure to make them resolve fully can have some strange effects. Finally, ensure your text's alignments are correct. Only use left-aligned text if this is truly your intention for every experience. For most uses, you should use natural alignment. This presents text left to right in most languages but will switch to right to left when needed.

When creating a new localization by pressing the + button in Figure 5-3, Xcode presents you with a dialog asking what action you'd like to take with each view file in your project. You have two options – a new view file and a localized strings file. The localized strings file will be the preferred option for most uses. See the next section on strings for more on how this works.

The more heavy-duty option is to create a new view file. This duplicates the existing file but allows you to make modifications to the views, not limited to the text values. You can use these files to modify how your views work for languages that are much shorter or longer than your development language, or those languages that are written in a different direction. Be aware that any changes you make to one view file are not reflected in any of the others, meaning if you're supporting five localizations, that's five Interface Builder files you're going to have to change. The good news is that different localizations can have different methods of localization. As an example, it's possible to support four localizations with strings files and just one with a new interface Builder file.

When creating a new view file, these are not localized by default. If you decide to localize, select the file in the navigator, and open the file inspector. Press the Localize button (Figure 7-8) to generate localized versions of this view.

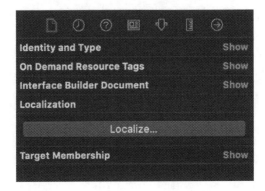

Figure 7-8. Xcode File Inspector's Localize button

Strings

Not all of your app's strings will be embedded in storyboards. For these, you'll need to create a Localizable.strings file. Visit File ➤ New ➤ File, and chose a Strings file. Call it Localizable.strings.

This file is a collection of key-value pairs for strings used in your app. The key can be in any string format you wish, but generally it's best practice to keep the format consistent within your app. Try to make it evident from a glance this is a key, not a string. And try to clarify where the string is used and for what purpose. For these reasons, I prefer the format of using all caps naming the screen first, then the purpose of the string, separated by a period (Listing 7-7). End each line with a semicolon, even if you're using Swift.

Listing 7-7. A localized value of "Listing Detail" used as the title for the app's detail page

```
"DETAIL_PAGE.TITLE" = "Listing Detail";
```

To use these strings in code, use NSLocalizedString as in Listing 7-8. This takes your strings key as an argument and a comment. Xcode provides the comment to your translator to guide them on how best to translate the meaning. Be aware that if your localized string cannot be found, the key is the string displayed to your customer. For this reason, you can optionally pass a value property to provide a default.

Listing 7-8. Setting the pageTitle UILabel's text using a localized string in code

```
pageTitle.text = NSLocalizedString("DETAIL_PAGE.TITLE",
value: "Listing Detail",
comment: "Header for the listing page")
```

LOCALIZING A PROJECT

Let's localize an existing project. If you haven't already, clone the GitHub repo for this book. Open Exercise 7-1 in Xcode. If it's not already selected, chose the project file from at the top of the project navigator. Then select the project in the editor pane.

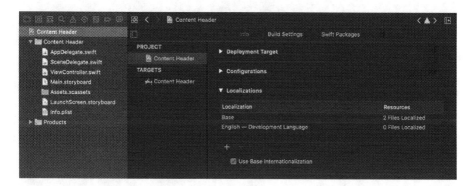

Figure 7-9. *Finding the demo project's localization settings*

You'll notice there are already two localizations (Figure 7-9). The base localization – the default; and English – my development language. Let's go ahead and add another. I'm going to use Google Translate to get values in German; you can do the same to choose whichever language you wish.

Caution   Never translate your apps using an automated service; always use a professional translation service.

Press the + button underneath Localizations and pick German (de) as seen in Figure 7-10.

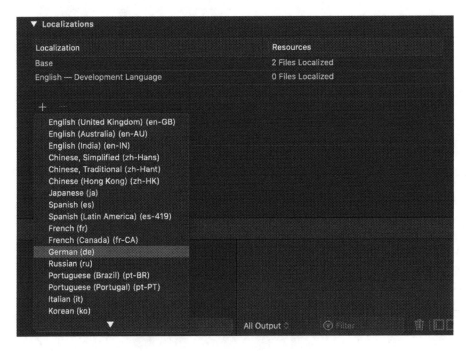

Figure 7-10. *Changing your scheme's language*

We're going to use strings files, so on the next screen (Figure 7-11), make sure both the storyboard files have the Localizable Strings option selected.

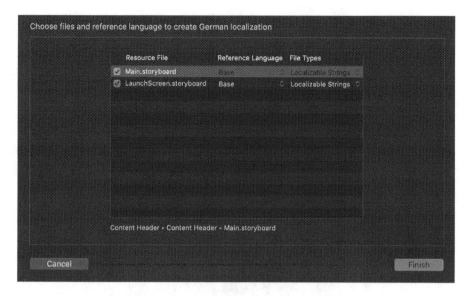

Figure 7-11. *Select all the files you want to localize, and choose "Localizable Strings"*

In the project navigator on the left, a disclosure indicator has now appeared next to both files. Open the one next to Main.storyboard, and notice there are two children (Figure 7-12), the base localization storyboard and a new strings file marked German.

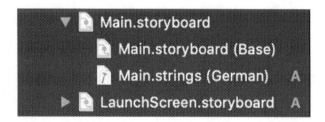

Figure 7-12. *The project navigator showing our localized storyboards*

First, let's take a look at the storyboard file to see what strings we have. This app is for booking holidays to space (Figure 7-13), each detail page gives us information about the space destination we can visit, along with a photo. Most of the text that will appear in this view will vary depending on the listing, so we haven't included them in this storyboard file. The only string we want to reuse across destinations is "Destination."

Figure 7-13. *Our holiday listing app showing the strings we need to localize*

Open the new strings file. Xcode has generated a key-value pair for the only string we have in the storyboard. Here, replace the word Destination with "Ziel."

The rest of our strings are set dynamically in code, so for those, we'll need a localized strings file. Go to File ➤ New ➤ File, and choose a strings file. Name this Localizable.strings. We have three strings we need to move into this file from ViewController.swift. Add these with suitable keys, such as the example in Listing 7-9.

Listing 7-9. An entry in a localizable strings file

```
"DETAIL_PAGE.MARS.HEADING" = "Mars";
```

Now we need to tell our view controller to use these new localized strings. Something like in Listing 7-10.

Listing 7-10. Accessing a localized string in code

```
pageTitle?.text = NSLocalizedString("DETAIL_PAGE.MARS.
HEADING",
value: "Mars",
comment: "Mars planet name")
```

Be sure to follow the two steps above for the other two strings giving each its own identifier. Once you have done this, we need to create a German localization of our strings file. Select the file in the project navigator, and open the file inspector. Press the "Localize…" button (Figure 7-8). Xcode will then ask which localization the existing file belongs to. Select English and press Localize. Back in the file inspector, you'll notice the Localize button has disappeared, and in its place is a list of your active localizations with a check next to English. Check German. A new file is created for you with the same content as the original. Here we can start to add our new German localized strings.

Mars in German is Mars. So let's delete the key-value pair for the heading as we'll just be using the default. Replace the subheading value with "Der Rote Planet," and replace the description too. I'll let you create your own translation here.

To run your app in German, without changing your device or simulator settings, edit your target's scheme (Figure 7-14). Under Run ➤ Options, there is a dropdown for Application Language (Figure 7-15).

Figure 7-14. *Edit your app's scheme to change the running language*

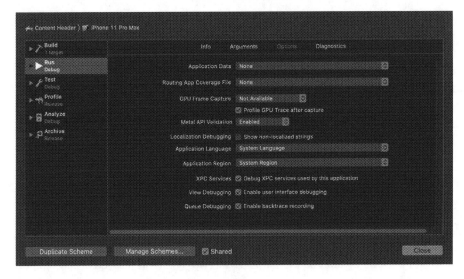

Figure 7-15. *Change the application's running language with the Application Language option*

Change this to German and close the window. On next run, your app will display your new German translation.

Summary

- Read Apple's Human Interface Guidelines. It's the last word in making your app feel at home on iOS for all of your users. Follow the advice Apple set out here, and you're more likely to have your app featured on the App Store and less likely to get an app review rejection.

- Enable the accessibility shortcut before continuing with the book, and keep it enabled even after you've finished reading. It gives you quick access to popular accessibility tools and will help with pain-free accessibility testing.

- Preparing your app for localization is good practice as it removes hard-coded strings from your code and makes it easier to change them in future. If you do them decide to localize your app, a bunch of work is already done.

- Even if your app is only available in one market you still stand to increase your market by localizing your app.

Over the next three chapters, we'll dive a little deeper into the accessibility features Apple has created to benefit people with specific disabilities or requirements. The following chapter will cover the broadest range of features; vision considerations.

CHAPTER 8

iOS Accessibility Features – Vision

The following features Apple primarily designed to assist people with visual impairments. These features help blind and low-vision users including long-sightedness, low vision, color impairments, blindness, and others. Some configurations can also be helpful to people with cognitive impairments, ADHD, low literacy, or people who prefer their text a little larger or their colors a little more muted. Some people enable the grayscale color filter just because it looks cool. Vision considerations make up the largest group of accessibility features currently available on iOS.

VoiceOver

The iOS accessibility feature with which devs are most likely familiar is VoiceOver. VoiceOver is Apple's built-in screen reader that features on all of their screen-based platforms and works with your app without requiring developers to enable its use. VoiceOver is far more than basic a screen reader; it also serves as a navigation tool for low-vision users to

© Rob Whitaker 2020
R. Whitaker, *Developing Inclusive Mobile Apps*,
https://doi.org/10.1007/978-1-4842-5814-9_8

enable them not just to know what text is on the screen but what buttons or actions are available to them. iOS also features a more basic screen reader for reading content only; this screen reader is referred to in iOS as Spoken Content, and we cover this later in the chapter under the sections "Speak Selection" and "Speak Screen."

Caution   Don't enable VoiceOver until you've read "Navigating with VoiceOver."

VoiceOver will change how your app functions, as your user will employ a series of swipes to navigate your app in a natural direction (top left to bottom right in English). A bounding box is drawn on the screen to add a visual highlight to the element currently selected (Figure 8-1). On selection, VoiceOver reads the element's information to the user in the following order: Accessibility Label ➤ Accessibility Value ➤ Accessibility Traits ➤ Accessibility Hint. Each of these four values is determined for you as part of your app's accessibility user interface, covered in Chapter 6, and can be customized by you if iOS is not able to determine the ideal, or indeed any, value.

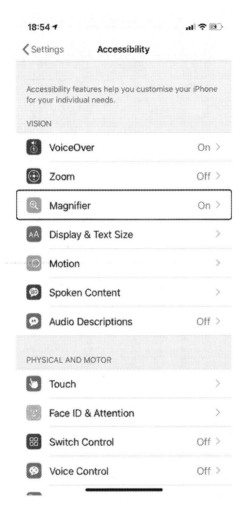

Figure 8-1. *VoiceOver selecting Magnifier. Double tap anywhere on the screen to activate this control*

While VoiceOver will do a large amount of work for you, it can be easy to create interfaces that aren't ideally compatible with VoiceOver. Common pitfalls include missing or incorrect accessibility values, labels, or traits; elements accessed in a nonlogical order; traps where VoiceOver cannot access or leave elements by swiping; and VoiceOver becoming out of sync with your UI. For these reasons, it is essential to check over your screens with VoiceOver when creating them, to ensure you can navigate as expected. Remember too that VoiceOver users will not have the full-screen context that a sighted person would; their only context is the currently selected element, so each element must make sense on its own. Semantic views covered in Chapter 6 are an excellent solution for this contextual problem.

You can check if VoiceOver is currently running by checking isVoiceOverRunning and determine if this status changes by listening to voiceOverStatusDidChangeNotification as per the example in Listing 8-1.

Listing 8-1. Detecting VoiceOver status and changes

```
import UIKit

class MyViewController: UIViewController {

    var voiceOverStatus: Bool {
        get{
            return UIAccessibility.isVoiceOverRunning }
    }

    override func viewDidLoad() {
        super.viewDidLoad()

        NotificationCenter.default.addObserver(self, selector:
        #selector(voiceOverChanged), UIAccessibility.
        voiceOverStatusDidChangeNotification, object: nil)
    }

    @objc
    func voiceOverChanged() {
      // check voiceOverStatus for the current status.
    }
}
```

Screen Updates

One common VoiceOver pitfall in UIKit is updating elements on a screen after iOS pushes the screen onto the view hierarchy. VoiceOver can't always know your view has changed, so it may not find new elements or may read old content. In SwiftUI this is no longer a consideration, but for UIKit you should always post a notification to UIAccessibility. On receiving this notification, the accessibility API will rebuild the accessible user interface to take the change into account. If you have changed a single element, post the layoutChanged notification (Listing 8-3), or, for a larger area of the screen, screenChanged (Listing 8-2). With each of these notifications, you can include an argument. This argument can be either a string for VoiceOver to announce or an element on which VoiceOver should focus.

Listing 8-2. Posting VoiceOver Change Notification for a major screen change

```
func updateSearchResults(results: Results) {
    // update your table view.

    ...

    let firstCell = tableView.cellForRow(at: IndexPath
    (row: 0, section: 0))

    // Focuses VoiceOver on the first cell.
    UIAccessibility.post(notification: .screenChanged,
    argument: firstCell)
}
```

Listing 8-3. Posting VoiceOver Change Notification for a screen layout change

```
func deleteItem(item: Item) {
    // handle removing the item from your screen.

    ...

    // VoiceOver announces "One item removed" and the
        accessibility user interface is recreated to reflect this.
    // VoiceOver focus is unchanged, unless the focus was on
        the removed element.
    UIAccessibility.post(notification: .layoutChanged,
    argument: "One item removed")
}
```

It is also possible to send announcements directly to VoiceOver in response to events when UI is unchanged. For example, in Listing 8-4, a warning or error that would not usually interrupt your user, such as where you might choose to display a toast.

Listing 8-4. Posting a VoiceOver announcement

```
func reachabilityFailed() {
    // display a toast informing of poor network connectivity.

    ...

    // VoiceOver announces "Warning: Poor network connectivity
        detected".
    // No changes are made to the accessibility user interface
        or VoiceOver focus.
    UIAccessibility.post(notification: .announcement,
    argument: "Warning: Poor network connectivity detected")
}
```

Posting a notification in this way will interrupt any current utterances. So it's best if you use this technique only when absolutely necessary. As an alternative, we can tell VoiceOver we want it to make an announcement only after it has finished its current utterance using an attributed string (Listing 8-5).

Listing 8-5. Posting a queued announcement

```
func reachabilityFailed() {
    // display a toast informing of poor network connectivity.

    ...

    let announcement = NSAttributedString(string: "Warning:
    Poor network connectivity detected", attributes:
    [.accessibilitySpeechQueueAnnouncement: true])

        UIAccessibility.post(notification: .announcement,
        argument: announcement)
```

In return, `UIAccessibility` will post a notification named `UIAccessibility.announcementDidFinishNotification` to `notificationCenter` once it has completed reading your announcement.

Attributed Accessibility Strings

Much like attributed strings for displaying rich text visually, we can also add attributes to our accessibility strings. Instead of controlling things like color and underline, these attributes control things like whether to include punctuation when speaking. Each of the label, hint, and value that make up our accessibility user interface can have attributes. These properties are `accessibilityAttributedLabel`, `accessibilityAttributedHint`, and `accessibilityAttributedValue`. We can also pass attributed strings to the VoiceOver notifications we covered above. Attributes we can add are as follows.

Pitch

The accessibilitySpeechPitch (Listing 8-6) key allows us to provide an NSNumber float value from 0.0 to 2.0. This value adjusts the vocal pitch that VoiceOver uses to read this text. 1.0 represents the user's chosen VoiceOver pitch, < 1.0 lowers the pitch, and > 1.0 raises the pitch. This can be useful for adding emphasis to a section of speech.

Listing 8-6. Adjusting VoiceOver pitch for emphasis

```
let attributedString = NSMutableAttributedString(string: "This
is the best app on the App Store!")

// Always localize your strings and perform proper range
    calculations. I'm hard-coding values here for brevity.
let range = NSRange(location: 12, length: 4)
        attributedString.addAttributes([.
        accessibilitySpeechPitch: 1.5], range: range)

appDescription?.accessibilityAttributedLabel = attributedString
```

Language

This key, accessibilitySpeechLanguage (Listing 8-7), allows us to specify a BCP 47[1] language key to define the language rules used for pronouncing a string. This can be used to provide more accurate pronunciation for non-native words.

Listing 8-7. Setting VoiceOver language for an foreign language word

```
spanishGreeting?.accessibilityAttributedLabel =
NSAttributedString(string: "Hola!", attributes:
[.accessibilitySpeechLanguage: "es-419"])
```

---

[1]http://www.rfc-editor.org/rfc/bcp/bcp47.txt

Spell Out

Spell Out reads each character of the string individually. From my own testing, this doesn't play well with capitalized words on iOS 13.

The accessibilitySpeechSpellOut (Listing 8-8) key is beneficial for when your app contains numbers such as account numbers or phone numbers. When VoiceOver encounters numbers, it makes a decision whether to read these as whole numbers or digits; from my experience, this decision is not always the correct one. Applying this attribute means VoiceOver will always read each figure individually.

Listing 8-8. Telling VoiceOver to read an account number as digits

```
let attributedString = NSMutableAttributedString(string: "Your
account number is 12345678")

// Always localize your strings and perform proper range
    calculations. I'm hard-coding values here for brevity.
let range = NSRange(location: 23, length: 8)
        attributedString.addAttributes
        ([.accessibilitySpeechSpellOut: true], range: range)

accountNumber?.accessibilityAttributedLabel = attributedString
```

Phonetic Notation

VoiceOver doesn't always have the correct pronunciation for every word, especially if this word is a brand name, for example. Using International Phonetic Alphabet, or IPA, notation we can specify to VoiceOver exactly how we want something pronounced. The key for this is accessibilitySpeechIPANotation (Listing 8-9).

Listing 8-9. Using IPA notation to specify pronunciation of AirBnB

```
brandName.accessibilityAttributedLabel = NSMutableAtt
ributedString(string: "[air-bee-an-bee]", attributes:
[.accessibilitySpeechIPANotation: true])
```

Punctuation

If your app contains code, or some other text where punctuation is important, you can use accessibilitySpeechPunctuation (Listing 8-10) to force VoiceOver to read each individual punctuation mark.

Listing 8-10. Requesting VoiceOver to announce punctuation for code

```
helloWorld.accessibilityAttributedLabel = NSMutableAttribu
tedString(string: "print(\"Hello, World!\")", attributes:
[.accessibilitySpeechPunctuation: true])
```

Magic Tap

Magic Tap is a fast way for accessibility users to access an important action on your screen. For example, in the timer app, Magic Tap starts or stops a timer. VoiceOver users perform a magic tap by double tapping anywhere on the screen with two fingers. You can add a Magic Tap to your View Controller or a subview. Adding this to a subview will mean the action is only performed when this view is focused. The standard use for a Magic Tap is to add this to your View Controller; this way the action will be performed regardless of the element that is in focus.

Support a magic tap gesture by overriding the accessibilityPerformMagicTap() function (Listing 8-11). You should then call whatever you consider your screen's primary purpose. Then return true, or false, if this wasn't possible.

Listing 8-11. Supporting Magic Tap

```
override func accessibilityPerformMagicTap() -> Bool {
    // perform your screen's main action

    return true // return false if the action failed
}
```

NAVIGATING WITH VOICEOVER

VoiceOver does not require enabling first; once you toggle this on in settings, VoiceOver is active. VoiceOver changes how navigating your iPhone works, so it's important not to turn it on and go tapping around without knowing how you can disable it first. Many times, when I was working at an Apple reseller, customers would bring in iPhones they hadn't been able to use for days, as idle thumbs had led them to enable VoiceOver and they weren't able to turn it off again. I even heard of people who wiped their phone entirely in an attempt to disable it.

Voiceover detects accessible elements in the natural order of your user's language setting – top left to bottom right in English – and highlights one element at a time. A single tap no longer activates the item, like you would expect when tapping a button, but instead tapping causes the element to be read. The screen can also be navigated by swiping, as elements may not always be visible or large enough for partially sighted people to accurately tap. So instead a swipe right will move to the element next toward the bottom right; a swipe left will navigate toward the top left. This element will then become active and will be read.

To activate an element – toggle a switch, tap a button, etc. –the gesture now becomes a double tap. The button will respond to this double tap, regardless of where on the screen you tap and what is under your finger when you tap. This is beneficial to people with visual impairments, as they may struggle to determine the accurate location of a tap target – so eliminating this requirement means more precise activation of controls. It also facilitates the use of the screen curtain. The screen curtain blanks out the iPhone's screen entirely, so the phone looks to anyone else as if the phone is asleep. As well as saving battery, this also provides extra privacy for blind and visually impaired users. As well as having their personal content read aloud, blind users may not be aware of the full content of the screen. This could end up inadvertently displaying sensitive personal information to those around them.

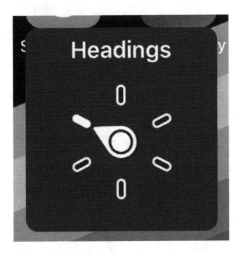

Figure 8-2. *The VoiceOver Rotor control selecting headings*

The rotor control (Figure 8-2) can be used to configure how a secondary VoiceOver gesture behaves. Swiping vertically rather than horizontally will perform the function chosen on the rotor. One of the most common uses is the headings option, this feature will skip content and only read elements marked with the accessibility trait of heading when swiping vertically on the screen. This is helpful to skim the content of a screen without having to navigate through every element. Other rotor controls let you navigate by accessibility actions, containers, control the speaking rate, or split up the text by reading single characters or words.

Zoom

Screen zoom is useful for people experiencing tunnel vision. But you may find other people use it if your dynamic text support is wanting or voiceover isn't clear about what content is on the screen. When you perform user testing, if you find visually impaired participants are firing up zoom on a specific screen, you may find this is because you need to make other accessibility improvements here.

Figure 8-3. *Zoom enabled in window mode*

Zoom can be used in one of two modes: firstly window zoom, where a viewfinder appears on the screen magnifying the content underneath (Figure 8-3). This mimics using a magnifying glass against the screen but without showing the underlying RGB pixels you'd see with a real-world magnifying glass. Secondly, full-screen zoom, where the entire screen is zoomed, and no longer fits the whole device's display.

Here's what makes it a secondary choice for some visually impaired users – either mode effectively cuts down what is displayed to your customer to around a quarter of the full-screen real estate. Meaning three-quarters of your screen's content is no longer visible, most notably content on the non-natural side (right in English). To use zoom you're required to move a finger around the screen to follow content, making elements easy to miss, and what content can be seen loses context. The content also then becomes pixelated and blurry, so it is harder to determine.

Zoom also features HUD (Figure 8-4) that allows easy control of the zoom region – full screen or windowed, ease of positioning the zoomed area, the ability to change zoom level, and the option to add a color filter to the zoomed area only. The final choice is excellent for people who find that a color filter helps them to see content but don't require the filter to be always enabled.

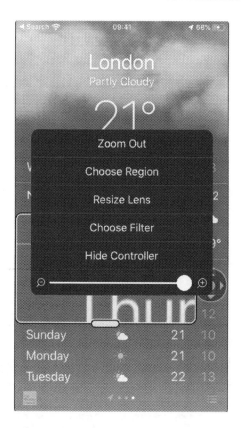

Figure 8-4. *Zoom HUD options*

Screen zoom will, by default, follow the focus on the screen, meaning if your customer is filling out a form, Zoom will move to the next text field as the cursor does. Sometimes, especially if you are using custom controls, this may not happen as seamlessly as you might like. In this case, you can use zoomFocusChanged(zoomType: .insertionPoint, toFrame: myCGRect, in: myUIView) (Listing 8-12) to inform Zoom that it should change focus to a certain area of your screen, where myCGRect is the area to focus on.

Listing 8-12. Moving Zoom focus to a view on viewDidAppear

```
import UIKit

Class MyViewController: UIViewController {
```

```
@IBOutlet private var myCustomView: CustomView!

override func viewDidAppear(_ animated: Bool) {
    super.viewDidAppear(animated)

    UIAccessibility.zoomFocusChanged(zoomType:
    .insertionPoint, toFrame: myCustomView.frame, in: view)
  }
}
```

To move the zoomed area around your screen, three-finger swipes are used, meaning that if you employ three-finger gestures at all in your app, these won't be consumed by zoom and not passed to your app. Unlike most accessibility features, Apple doesn't provide a property for your app to determine if zoom is enabled and to change behavior if required. Instead, you can use `registerGestureConflictWithZoom()` on a screen to prompt iOS to present a system alert (Figure 8-5) informing your customer that zoom may conflict with the functionality of your app; this alert allows your user to disable zoom.

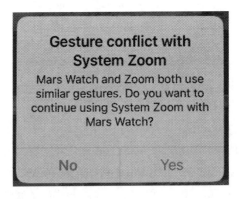

Figure 8-5. Zoom gesture conflict dialog presented when `registerGestureConflictWithZoom()` is called and the user has Zoom enabled

Bold Text

Bold text does what it says on the tin (Figure 8-6). If you are using UIFontTextStyles, your text will get this for free. If you have chosen not to use Apple's text styles, you should listen to isBoldTextEnabled and boldTextStatusDidChangeNotification (Listing 8-13) and switch to a bold font or add a bold attribute if requested. You may also want to consider switching any assets or increasing the weight of borders to make elements stand out more.

Listing 8-13. Detecting Bold Text status changes

```
import UIKit

class MyViewController: UIViewController {

    var boldTextStatus: Bool {
        get{
            return UIAccessibility.isBoldTextEnabled
        }
    }

    override func viewDidLoad() {
        super.viewDidLoad()

        NotificationCenter.default.addObserver(self, selector:
        #selector(boldTextChanged), name: UIAccessibility.
        boldTextStatusDidChangeNotification, object: nil)
    }

    @objc
    func boldTextChanged() {
      // check boldTextStatus for current status.
      // switch to bold fonts or assets as appropriate
    }
}
```

Figure 8-6. *iOS text styles with standard text (left) and bold text (right)*

Larger Text or Dynamic Type

Larger text is the friendly human-readable name for what we as devs would refer to as dynamic type. Dynamic type allows the user to adjust the text size to one better suited to how they use their device (Figure 8-7). In the manner of the best accessibility features, this isn't just about people who need larger text to be able to read the screen but about customization. This feature allows text sizes below the default, allowing more content to be fitted to the screen without scrolling. This can range from xSmall (extra small) with a body text size or 14pt to AX5 (accessibility size 5) with a body text size of 53. See Table 8-1 for the full range of body text point sizes.

Table 8-1. *Dynamic Type text sizes*

Dynamic type size	Body text size (points)
xSmall	14
Small	15
Medium	16
Large (Default)	17
xLarge	19
xxLarge	21
xxxLarge	23
AX1	28
AX2	33
AX3	40
AX4	47
AX5	53

The full range of dynamic text sizes matched to text styles are available as part of the HIG.[2]

Dynamic Type works best when used with iOS' built-in text styles, UIFontTextStyle. These styles tell iOS and the Dynamic Type system

---

[2]https://developer.apple.com/design/human-interface-guidelines/ios/ visual-design/typography/

221

what the semantic use of specific text is, meaning all your text is scaled in proportion, at Apple-recommended intervals. The full options for text styles are shown at different size settings here.

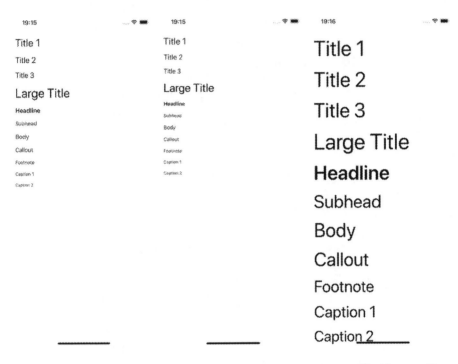

Figure 8-7. *Dynamic Type text styles at standard sizes (left), smallest sizes (center), and the largest accessibility size (right)*

As a general rule, all of your text should use one of these built-in text styles, Listing 8-14 shows how to achieve this in UIKit. In SwiftUI all text supports dynamic type and is styled as body by default. Additional styles can be chosen with the `.font()` modifier (Listing 8-15) and passing one of the dynamic type styles. Passing a defined size, such as `.system(size: 17)`, will disable dynamic type and prevent scaling, so should be avoided.

Listing 8-14. Creating labels with Dynamic Type in UIKit

```
let label = UILabel()
label.font = UIFont.preferredFont(forTextStyle: .body)
label.adjustsFontForContentSizeCategory = true
```

Listing 8-15. Creating labels with Dynamic Type in SwiftUI

```
// For body style, no font modifier is required.
Text("Example text").font(.headline)
```

To enable Dynamic Type in Interface Builder (Figure 8-8), open the attributes inspector, and select the "T" icon in the Font attribute box. Then click the new Font dropdown that appears and select your chosen text style. Finally, check the box underneath labeled "Automatically Adjusts Font."

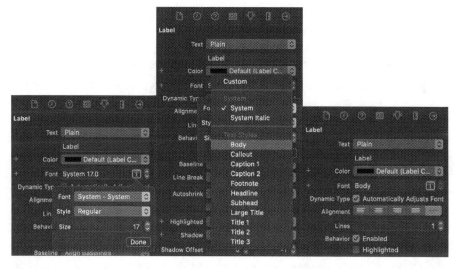

Figure 8-8. *Selecting a Dynamic Type text style in Interface Builder*

Custom Styles

What if your design calls for a font other than the iOS default, San Francisco? Or what if you want your standard body text size to be larger than 17? We can do this using iOS' UIFontMetrics (Listing 8-16). I won't cover adding custom fonts to your app here, but Apple provides a simple guide in their developer documentation.[3] Once you have your custom font ready, create a font instance in code with your font and the size you want it to be when text is set at the standard size. Create an instance of UIFontMetrics with the text style you're using this font for, then pass your custom font instance to your UIFontMetrics instance.

Listing 8-16. Creating a dynamic text style with a custom font

```
let font = UIFont(name: myCustomFontName, size: defaultSize)
let bodyMetrics = UIFontMetrics(forTextStyle: .body)
label.font = bodyMetrics.scaledFont(for: font)
label.adjustsFontForContentSizeCategory = true
```

Creating a text style in this way ensures you are respecting your customer's chosen text size. Plus, Apple configures line spacing, paragraph spacing, and other metrics for you, ensuring your text is always readable.

Button Shapes

Button shapes help make button tap targets more visible by variously adding an outline, background, or underlined text (Figure 8-9). For those without visual impairments, button shapes also make it simpler to determine which areas of the screen can be interacted with. If you have customized your buttons in any way, you may sometimes find text or button

---

[3]https://developer.apple.com/documentation/uikit/text_display_and_fonts/ adding_a_custom_font_to_your_app

shapes are misaligned. It's worth enabling these to check your app still looks OK and the button labels are still readable. If you're using an element as a button that isn't subclassed from `UIButton`, you won't get this behavior.

Figure 8-9. *Back navigation button with Button Shapes enabled*

On/Off Labels

For iOS' switch or toggle controls, Apple's design uses color only to indicate to your user whether your switch is on or off, meaning any person with a visual impairment which causes them to struggle differentiating colors can find it hard to understand this control. For this reason, Apple provides a setting to add labels to the switch – I when in the on position and O in the off position as shown in Figure 8-10.

Figure 8-10. *Switch controls with On/Off labels enabled*

When creating your own custom controls, you should consider this too, and if you choose not to use labels by default, listen to `isOnOffSwitchLabelsEnabled` and `onOffSwitchLabelsDidChangeNotification` (Listing 8-17) to decide when to add additional information.

Listing 8-17. Detecting changes in switch label status

```
import UIKit

class MyViewController: UIViewController {

    var switchLabelStatus: Bool {
        get{
            return UIAccessibility.isOnOffSwitchLabelsEnabled
        }
    }

    override func viewDidLoad() {
        super.viewDidLoad()

        NotificationCenter.default.addObserver(self, selector:
        #selector(switchLabelsChanged), name: UIAccessibility.
        onOffSwitchLabelsDidChangeNotification, object: nil)
    }

    @objc
    func switchLabelsChanged() {
      // check switchLabelStatus for current status
      // add on/off labels to your controls as needed.
    }
}
```

Reduce Transparency

Reduce Transparency is an essential feature for some low-vision users; for those with vision already blurred, adding blur on otherwise transparent backgrounds can make it challenging to determine foreground from background. Transparency can also cause the contrast ratio to fall below an acceptable value if the background is not defined at build time.

The most immediately noticeable use of this is folders on springboard (Figure 8-11). These are a great example of how to make an accessibility feature with comparable experience, rather than a second-class experience. With this feature disabled, folders have a light-gray transparent background; tap on the folder, and the background behind the transparent gray folder squircle is an untinted blurred springboard. Enable this setting, and the springboard content is removed when accessing a folder, keeping a dimmed springboard background image. Folders take on a darker gray appearance with no transparency, but the gray background color has a hint of the color of the springboard background image behind it.

Figure 8-11. *SpringBoard folder (Left). SpringBoard folder with reduced transparency (Right)*

Reduce transparency is not enabled for you by default in the same manner as many of the text accommodations, as Apple can't make a clear decision on how to reduce transparency based on your UI design. If you are using transparency in your design, the decision on whether and how to respond to this setting must be yours. If your transparency layer is above a solid color that you can guarantee will not change from build time, there may be no need to respond at all. In all other cases, some compromise should be made. An easy decision would be to replace transparency with a solid color; a better choice may be to make a comparable experience such as in Apple's Springboard folders, where a tint of the background image is used.

To determine whether to respond to this setting, use iOS' Accessibility API, and access the isReduceTransparencyEnabled variable, and listen to reduceTransparencyStatusDidChangeNotification as in Listing 8-18 below.

Listing 8-18. Detecting changes in Reduce Transparency status

```
import UIKit

class MyViewController: UIViewController {

    var reduceTransparencyStatus: Bool {
        get{
            return UIAccessibility.isReduceTransparencyEnabled
        }
    }

    override func viewDidLoad() {
        super.viewDidLoad()

        NotificationCenter.default.addObserver(self,
        selector: #selector(reduceTransparencyChanged),
        name: UIAccessibility.reduceTransparencyStatusDidChange
        Notification, object: nil)
    }
```

```
@objc
func reduceTransparencyChanged() {
  // check reduceTransparencyStatus for current status.
  // add opacity to views as needed.
  }
}
```

Increase Contrast

Increase Contrast is the user-friendly name for UIAccessibility's darker system colors option. Darker system colors, however, is a more descriptive name for what this option actually does – inbuilt Apple apps will darken colors, especially those behind text, to increase contrast (Figure 8-12). Toggle this option in settings, and see the tint on the top back button change; also navigate to Messages and note the difference in the color of the message bubbles.

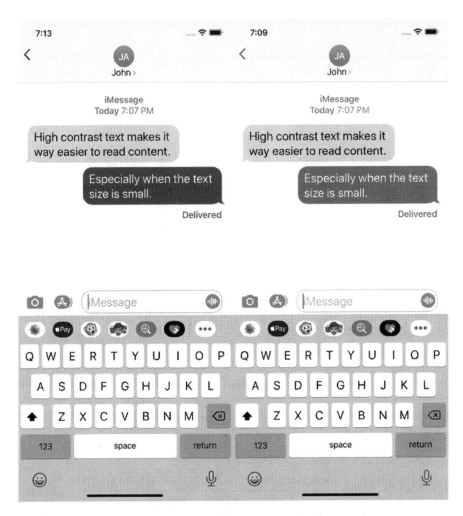

Figure 8-12. *Increase Contrast in Messages (left) and the feature toggled off (right). Note darker text in the message compose field and darker backgrounds on message bubbles*

To determine whether to respond to this setting, use iOS' Accessibility API, and access the isDarkerSystemColorsEnabled variable, and listen to darkerSystemColorsStatusDidChangeNotification (Listing 8-19). From iOS 13, this setting can also be determined from the view's trait collection

with the accessibilityContrast property (Listing 8-20). The trait
returns an enum with the value of either normal or high, reflecting your
customer's setting.

Listing 8-19. Detecting if increase contrast is enabled

```
import UIKit

class MyViewController: UIViewController {

    var darkerColorsStatus: Bool {
        get{
            return UIAccessibility.isDarkerSystemColorsEnabled
        }
    }

    override func viewDidLoad() {
        super.viewDidLoad()

        NotificationCenter.default.addObserver(self, selector:
        #selector(darkerColorsChanged), name: UIAccessibility.
        darkerSystemColorsStatusDidChangeNotification, object:
        nil)
    }

    @objc
    func darkerColorsChanged() {
      // check darkerColorsStatus for current status
      // replace colors/assets for high contrast alternatives
    }
}
```

Listing 8-20. Determining high-contrast status from a view's trait collection

```
let contrast = traitCollection.accessibilityContrast
// returns an enum value of .high or .normal.
```

Switching colors is handled for you by iOS so long as you have provided your app with a high-contrast variant. Image and color assets stored in an asset catalog can both have a high-contrast variant supplied (Figure 8-13). Open your xcassets file, and select the color or image resource for which you want to create a high-contrast variant. From the attributes inspector on the right, toggle the "High Contrast" checkbox. A second variant will appear for each asset value selected. iOS will automatically choose the appropriate asset for you based on your customer's setting. Any colors or images not stored in an asset catalog will need to be switched in your code after determining the status of this setting as in Listing 8-11.

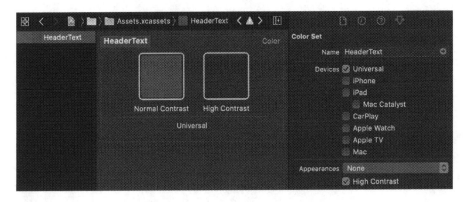

Figure 8-13. *Normal and High Contrast color variants in an asset catalog*

Differentiate Without Color

Some impairments, such as color blindness, can hinder our ability to perceive colors. As such, a key feature of WCAG is to provide information to your customer in multiple redundant forms. For example, a red warning triangle containing an exclamation, grouped with the label "Error," is providing the information to your customer in three ways – shape, color, and text.

Sometimes your designs might call for the use of color alone such as coloring text labels or backgrounds to hint at different statuses. If your app is using color in this way, its meaning could easily be lost to anyone who experiences color differently.[4]

To determine if you should be providing additional forms of furnishing this information, listen to `shouldDifferentiateWithoutColor` and `differentiateWithoutColorDidChangeNotification`, see Listing 8-21.

Listing 8-21. Detecting changes in differentiate without color status

```
import UIKit

class MyViewController: UIViewController {

    var differentiateWithoutColorStatus: Bool {
        get{
            return UIAccessibility.shouldDifferentiateWithoutColor
        }
    }

    override func viewDidLoad() {
        super.viewDidLoad()
```

---

[4]Remember also that if you are changing background or text color in this way, each possible color combination should pass the WGAG guideline of at least 4.5:1 contrast ratio.

```
        NotificationCenter.default.addObserver(self, selector:
        #selector(differentiateWithoutColorChanged), name:
        NSNotification.Name(rawValue: UIAccessibility.
        differentiateWithoutColorDidChangeNotification), object:
        nil)
    }

    @objc
    func differentiateWithoutColorChanged() {
        // check differentiateWithoutColorStatus for current status.
        // Add shapes or text to add meaning.
    }
}
```

Invert Colors

Inverting colors helps to improve contrast, as where most apps would usually be displayed as dark text on a light background; flipping that provides lighter text on a dark background causing the text to stand out (Figure 8-14). It is also used by those who have light or color sensitivity, as it has the effect of reducing the amount of bright color on the screen.

Classic invert changes everything, meaning your images will often look entirely wrong. With smart invert, iOS uses some judgement of what is present on the screen to decide whether to invert the colors or not. In general, text content and backgrounds are inverted, while images and videos are kept in standard color. iOS is not 100% successful on this; in general, if you have placed content over an image, that image will usually be inverted. Some screens don't change at all, along with some tint colors. To get a better understanding of what Smart Invert does, I'd recommend enabling this feature and navigating your device for a while. Notice the difference in particular images, tint colors, etc., whereas many stay the same.

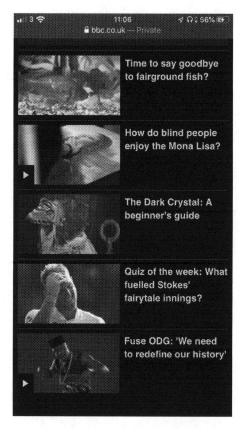

Figure 8-14. *Smart invert – text and backgrounds are inverted; images are kept at their original color*

If you find parts of your app that would work better when not inverted, UIView includes a property for accessibilityIgnoresInvertColors (Listing 8-22). This property can be set to true to ensure your colors stay the same regardless of the user's device setting. The property will prevent inversion on the view where this is set and all of its subviews. Use this property wisely; setting this to true on every view might keep designers happy but will likely anger your customer who chose to enable the setting to help them use your app. Use this property for usability, not for the sake of design.

Listing 8-22. Setting an image to ignore the inverted color setting

```
// heroImage is a reference to a UIImageView on our screen
heroImage.accessibilityIgnoresInvertColors = true
```

Color Filters

Color filters allow your customers to adjust how certain or all colors appear, making determining different colors easier for those who might struggle with contrast or color. These filters can also be used to reduce the vibrancy of colors or switch off color entirely. There is no change required to your app and no setting to listen to detect these filters, but it is worth being aware that some of your customers may choose to use these filters and that they will change the appearance of your app.

Most filters do not report to your app if they are enabled, but grayscale can be detected using isGrayscaleEnabled and grayscaleStatusDidChangeNotification (Listing 8-23).

Listing 8-23. Detecting changes in Grayscale status

```
import UIKit

class MyViewController: UIViewController {

    var grayscaleStatus: Bool {
        get{
            return UIAccessibility.isGrayscaleEnabled
        }
    }

    override func viewDidLoad() {
        super.viewDidLoad()
```

```swift
    NotificationCenter.default.addObserver(self, selector:
    #selector(grayscaleChanged), name: UIAccessibility.
    grayscaleStatusDidChangeNotification, object: nil)
  }

  @objc
  func grayscaleChanged() {
    // check grayscaleStatus for current status.
    // Add shapes or text to add meaning.
  }
}
```

Reduce White Point

Reduce White Point reduces the intensity of colors, adding a gray element to them; this reduces eye strain and causes less glare but may create a slight change in appearance for some of your UX or images. The difference is subtle, so providing you have made sure your designs have sufficient contrast, this shouldn't have a negative effect.

Reduce Motion

The Reduce Motion option is essential for people affected by motion, where specific animations can trigger dizziness and nausea. It's also invaluable for people with anxiety disorders, ADHD, and autism, among others. With these impairments, large amounts of motion, especially in the periphery, can be distracting and upsetting. To get an idea of the kind of animations that can trigger, enable this option on your phone. As you use your phone keep, an eye out for which animations Apple has disabled, the zooming animation when launching an app, for example. Fast animations, animations in multiple plains, and zooming animations can all have an effect, so if you make use of these, consider listening to isReduceMotionEnabled before triggering an animation, and use an alternative form of presentation. The notification posted when this setting is changed is reduceMotionStatusDidChangeNotification (Listing 8-24).

Listing 8-24. Detecting if Reduce Motion is enabled

```
import UIKit

class MyViewController: UIViewController {

    var reduceMotionStatus: Bool {
        get{
            return UIAccessibility.isReduceMotionEnabled
        }
    }

    override func viewDidLoad() {
        super.viewDidLoad()

        NotificationCenter.default.addObserver(self, selector:
        #selector(reduceMotionChanged), name: UIAccessibility.
        reduceMotionStatusDidChangeNotification, object: nil)
    }

    @objc
    func reduceMotionChanged() {
      // check reduceMotionStatus for current status.
      // stop or reduce the intensity of animation.
    }
}
```

Speak Selection

Speak Selection adds an extra option to the pop-up ribbon when long pressing on a word or text selection. Additional to the standard options of Copy, Look Up, etc., a button for Speak appears (Figure 8-15). Tap it, and Siri will read only the highlighted word or selection. You can check if this is enabled with isSpeakSelectionEnabled and listen for changes in this setting with speakSelectionStatusDidChangeNotification (Listing 8-25).

Listing 8-25. Detecting changes in Speak Selection status

```
import UIKit

class MyViewController: UIViewController {

    var speakSelectionStatus: Bool {
        get{
            return UIAccessibility.isSpeakSelectionEnabled
        }
    }

    override func viewDidLoad() {
        super.viewDidLoad()

        NotificationCenter.default.addObserver(self,
        selector: #selector(speakSelectionChanged),
        name: UIAccessibility.speakSelectionStatusDidChange
        Notification, object: nil)
    }
```

```
@objc
func speakSelectionChanged() {
    // check speakSelectionStatus for current status.
    // pause any audio or video playing.
}
}
```

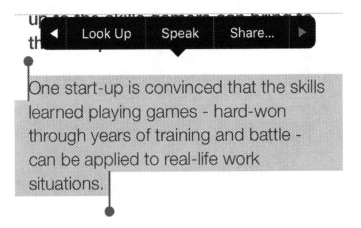

Figure 8-15. *Speak Selection*

Speak Screen

Speak Screen is the friendly name Apple uses for the iOS built-in screen reader. Speak Screen is far dumber than VoiceOver, as it doesn't feature any of the navigation or control functions. When enabled, Speak Screen (Figure 8-16) can be activated by swiping down from the top of the screen with two fingers. Speak Screen then identifies the content portions of your screen and reads them from top left to bottom right ignoring any navigation bar or tab bar buttons or titles.

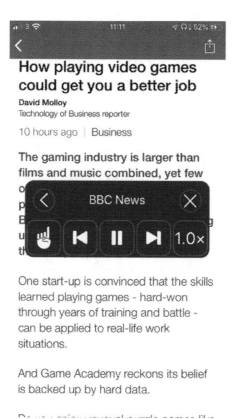

Figure 8-16. *Speak Screen*

Speak Screen respects the same `isAccessibilityElement` property used by VoiceOver and so will skip the same views and controls. The behavior is different from VoiceOver in that the user has no control over what is read and when meaning they can't choose to skip or repeat sections. It's worth enabling Speak Screen on your app and activating it on each screen to determine if your content makes sense when read in this way.

Speak Screen can be enabled in settings without making any changes to the look or behavior of the device. You can determine if this setting has been enabled by checking `isSpeakScreenEnabled`. Note that this property returning true doesn't mean Speak Screen has been activated on any of

your screens; speakScreenStatusDidChangeNotification can be used to
determine if your user changes this setting while using your app (Listing 8-26).

Listing 8-26. Detecting changes in Speak Screen status

```
import UIKit

class MyViewController: UIViewController {

    var speakScreenStatus: Bool {
        get{
            return UIAccessibility.isSpeakScreenEnabled
        }
    }

    override func viewDidLoad() {
        super.viewDidLoad()

        NotificationCenter.default.addObserver(self, selector:
        #selector(speakScreenChanged), name: UIAccessibility.
        speakScreenStatusDidChangeNotification, object: nil)
    }

    @objc
    func speakScreenChanged() {
      // check speakScreenStatus for current status.
      // pause any audio or video playing.
    }
}
```

Speak Screen will continue reading all available content on the
screen until it reaches the bottom; it will then attempt to scroll to find
more content to read. If it is unable to scroll, scrolling is attempted on the
parent view and so on, until there are no further parent views; at this point
reading stops. Any naturally scrolling UIKit elements will implement this

scrolling for you. If you are scrolling by any other means – such as turning a page in an eBook or swiping right to the left in a series of onboarding screens, you should implement theaccessibilityScroll(_ direction: UIAccessibilityScrollDirection) function as in Listing 8-27. If scrolling is successful, you must return true and post the pageScrolled accessibility notification.

Listing 8-27. Accessibility Scrolling

```
import UIKit

class MyViewController: UIViewController {

    override func accessibilityScroll(_ direction:
    UIAccessibilityScrollDirection) -> Bool {
        if lastPage() {
            return false
        }

        present(nextPage(), animated: true) {
            UIAccessibility.post(notification: .pageScrolled,
                                 argument: nil)
        }

        return true
    }

    func nextPage() -> UIViewController {
        // return your next content view controller
        return NextViewController()
    }
```

```
    func lastPage() -> Bool {
       // return true if this is the last page of this content
       if isLastPage {
          return true
       }

       return false
    }
}
```

Audio Descriptions

AVFoundation contains built-in support audio description tracks. Using an AVPlayer instance for your media will give you this functionality for free when your customer has this setting enabled – providing you ensure your videos have audio description embedded in your video. Any good video-editing software will allow you to add secondary audio tracks for descriptions.

Dark Mode

Dark Mode is a new feature for iOS 13. Your app supports Dark Mode right out of the box without requiring any changes. But if you haven't made changes the chances are your app is going to look a bit weird with Dark Mode enabled. Dark mode, while also looking neat and saving battery life, is an essential accessibility feature for people with light sensitivity, and the higher contrast helps with some visual impairments such as color deficiencies and blurred vision.

You can toggle Dark Mode through the Settings app under Display and Brightness (Figure 8-17). Toggle Dark Mode now and test out your app to see where you might need to make changes. You may need to add dark variants of some colors and image assets. We'll cover this below.

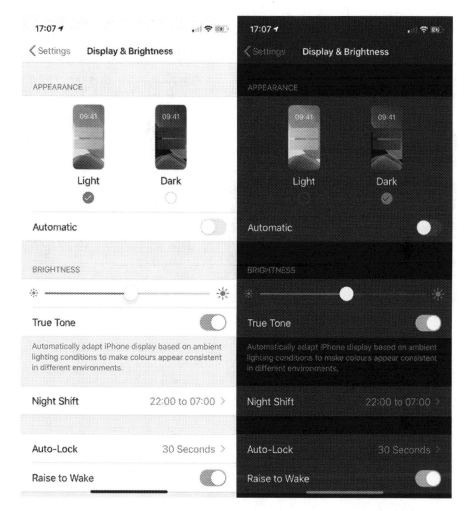

Figure 8-17. *Display and Brightness settings in Light Mode (Left)
and Dark Mode (right)*

Dark (or light) variants of colors and images can be added to any
assets stored in asset catalogs. Select the color or image you want to add a
dark variant of, and in the appearance section of the attributes inspector
choose "Any, Dark." (Figure 8-18) The "Any" asset is the value iOS will use
on devices before iOS 13, where Dark Mode is not a feature. Usually, this

would be the same as your "Light" option, but if you need to specify a light option as well as a legacy asset, choose the "Any, Light, Dark" option.

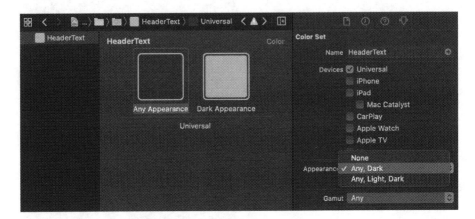

Figure 8-18. *Dark and Any color variants in an asset catalog*

If you need to make further UI changes based on the color mode, you can query your view's trait collection (Listing 8-28). `userInterfaceStyle` will return an enum value of `.light`, `.dark`, or. `.unspecified` for iOS versions below 13.

Listing 8-28. Checking Dark Mode status on a view

```
let darkMode = traitCollection.userInterfaceStyle
// Returns .light, .dark, or .unspecified as an enum value.
```

Summary

- Visual considerations make up by far the largest selection of iOS accessibility features, so it could feel daunting trying to support them all. But sticking with good practices – using iOS-provided controls, layout constraints, and asset catalogs – will go a long way.

- VoiceOver can seem confusing when you first use it, but you'll pick up the basics quickly and can make it a regular part of your development workflow.

- Dynamic Type is an essential part of any modern iOS app. If you don't support it, your app won't feel at home on iOS, and your customers will notice.

In the next chapter, we'll continue our look at iOS accessibility features. We'll move on to the considerations iOS makes for people with limited movement and cover what you can do as a developer to make these customers feel at home in your app.

iOS Accessibility Features – Physical and Motor

Physical and motor considerations assist people who struggle with multi-touch gestures; if, for example, someone had three fingers, they may need assistance to perform a four-finger gesture. Through to people who may have virtually no motor control at all, where switch control or voice control may help make the best use of what movement your user has available to them.

Assistive Touch

Assistive touch renders a small movable on-screen home button-like tap target (Figure 9-1), which expands to further options on tap (Figure 9-2 and Figure 9-3). This feature is excellent for people with motor issues, who might struggle to swipe for the control center, or people missing digits who would struggle to perform a pinch gesture, for example. The presence of this button does not affect the functionality of your app, but you should perhaps be aware that with this present, there will be a small area of your screen obscured by the Assistive Touch button.

© Rob Whitaker 2020
R. Whitaker, *Developing Inclusive Mobile Apps*,
https://doi.org/10.1007/978-1-4842-5814-9_9

Figure 9-1. *Assistive Touch partially obscuring content*

Worthy of higher consideration is your use of gestures that might require fine motor skills such as multi-finger taps, swipes, pinches, and other touch gestures. If your app makes use of these, consider monitoring isAssistiveTouchRunning, and offer an alternative. You can detect changes in this setting by listening to assistiveTouchStatusDidChangeNotification (Listing 9-1).

Listing 9-1. Detecting changes in Assistive Touch status

```
import UIKit

class MyViewController: UIViewController {

    var assistiveTouchStatus: Bool {
        get{
            return UIAccessibility.isAssistiveTouchRunning
        }
    }

    override func viewDidLoad() {
        super.viewDidLoad()
```

```
    NotificationCenter.default.addObserver(self,
    selector: #selector(assistiveTouchChanged), name:
    UIAccessibility.assistiveTouchStatusDidChange
    Notification, object: nil)
}

@objc
func assistiveTouchChanged() {
  // check assistiveTouchStatus for current status.
  // increase the prominence of gesture alternatives
}
}
```

Figure 9-2. *Assistive Touch providing single-tap access to features*

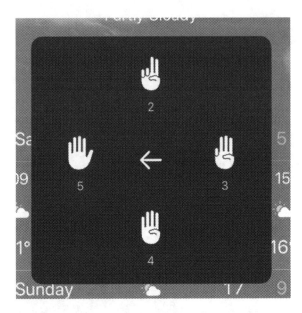

Figure 9-3. *Assistive Touch providing single-tap access to multi-finger gestures*

Shake to Undo

Shake to Undo is a system-wide undo command (Figure 9-4), the equivalent of ⌘ + Z or Edit ➤ Undo on the Mac. This feature can be difficult for people who struggle with motor skills and perhaps lack the movement in their hands to perform this gesture. Additionally, many people find they trigger Shake to Undo by accident, such as people with Parkinson's disease.

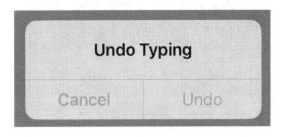

Figure 9-4. *iOS's standard Shake to Undo confirmation dialog. This modal dialog can be frustrating if triggered accidentally*

Your customer can disable this feature to prevent frustration from accidentally triggering the dialog. If the ability to undo is a crucial feature for your app, say if you provide text editing features, you may wish to add, or preferably increase the prominence of, an alternative undo mechanism. You can query isShakeToUndoEnabled to determine if shake to undo is available, and you can listen to the shakeToUndoDidChangeNotification for changes (Listing 9-2).

Listing 9-2. Detecting changes in Shake to Undo status

```
import UIKit

class MyViewController: UIViewController {

    var shakeToUndoStatus: Bool {
        get{
            return UIAccessibility.isShakeToUndoEnabled
        }
    }

    override func viewDidLoad() {
        super.viewDidLoad()

        NotificationCenter.default.addObserver(self, selector:
        #selector(shakeToUndoChanged), name: UIAccessibility.
        shakeToUndoDidChangeNotification, object: nil)
    }

    @objc
    func shakeToUndoChanged() {
      // check shakeToUndoStatus for current status.
      // increase the prominence of undo features.
    }
}
```

Switch Control

Switch Control is intended for use by those with more extreme motor impairments. While Assistive Touch can make certain gestures easier, Switch Control is designed for people who struggle to touch or tap at all.

Caution   Don't enable Switch Control until you have read "Navigating with Switch Control."

Using the accessibility user interface iOS has generated of your app, Switch Control will automatically scan the screen highlighting accessible elements with a bounding box, similar to the appearance of VoiceOver. The difference to VoiceOver here is that instead of highlighting every accessible element in turn, elements are automatically grouped into meaningful areas to reduce the number of presses required to access any given element. Content-only elements are also excluded, as this Switch Control is intended as a tool for allowing control; only elements that can be interacted with are highlighted. On selecting an element, the element's available actions are presented in a drop down (Figure 9-5). If you use iOS' built-in controls such as UIButton, these actions will be populated for you. But if you want to add an alternative to a gesture, a great option is to add an accessibility custom action here. Details of these are available in Chapter 6.

Figure 9-5. *Switch Control*

The purpose of this navigation method is to allow users with severely limited motion to be able to navigate their device using just one single gesture. However, more gestures can be added depending on the user's abilities. The switch in question can be many things. Your device's screen can make one single switch, or external physical switches can be connected using Made for iPhone switches or switch controllers. These can be connected by Bluetooth or MIDI over a USB to lightning adapter. For users who lack the motor ability to press or tap one of these physical switches, it is possible to use the device's camera to detect head movements, allowing left or right head movements to control different aspects of the device.

Navigating an interface in this way can be time-consuming. As a result, your users with Switch Control enabled are most likely to be the ones most impacted by time-outs.

You can detect the status of Switch Control by listening to switchControlStatusDidChangeNotification or by querying isSwitchControlRunning (Listing 9-3).

Listing 9-3. Detecting changes in Switch Control status

```swift
import UIKit

class MyViewController: UIViewController {

    var switchControlStatus: Bool {
        get{
            return UIAccessibility.isSwitchControlRunning
        }
    }

    override func viewDidLoad() {
        super.viewDidLoad()

        NotificationCenter.default.addObserver(self, selector:
        #selector(switchControlChanged), name: UIAccessibility.
        switchControlStatusDidChangeNotification, object: nil)
    }

    @objc
    func switchControlChanged() {
      // check switchControlStatus for current status.
      // increase the prominence of gesture alternatives.
    }
}
```

Navigation Style

When elements are highlighted by Switch Control, they are usually done individually. Depending on the layout, Switch Control may determine it is logical to group elements together, say in a grouped table view. We can adjust our accessibility interface to tell Switch Control that it should either always treat elements as a group or individually (Figure 9-6). Grouping elements allows for faster navigation to other areas of the UI. Treating them individually is appropriate for when controls are important. Getting the balance right here can be difficult and ideally would be judged with the help of some user testing with participants who use Switch Control daily.

Figure 9-6. *Navigating with Switch Control. Elements navigated separatley (left) and combined (right)*

Each view has a property of `accessibilityNavigationStyle`; we can set this to either `.separate` or `.combined` (Listing 9-4), depending on our desired outcome.

Listing 9-4. Setting the Switch Control navigation style to group elements presented in a Stack View

```
buttonStackView.accessibilityNavigationStyle = .combined
```

NAVIGATING WITH SWITCH CONTROL

Before enabling Switch Control, you need to add a switch to your device. Your screen is probably the simplest option for use in a testing situation, although I'd also recommend trying this out with using head movements and the front-facing camera. Under the Switch Control menu in Accessibility settings, tap Switches ➤ Add New Switch… ➤ Screen ➤ Full Screen ➤ Select Item.

Now enable Switch Control through the Accessibility settings, or in future by activating the Accessibility Shortcut we set up at the beginning of the section. You'll see a blue bounding box appear at the top of the screen; after a second, this box will move down the screen to the next group of selectable elements; after another second, the box will make another jump and so on. To activate the highlighted area, tap anywhere on the device's screen. If this highlight contains a group of items, the scanner will begin to cycle through the elements. Switch Control does this with a seconds interval.

Once you have used Switch Control to activate a single element, you are presented with a drop-down menu of possible actions. These actions are cycled through in the same method as the screen itself, meaning you can tap anywhere on the screen to perform the highlighted action or focus on the highlighted group to navigate toward a different action. The first action highlighted is always Tap, meaning a double tap on an element is effectively the same as tapping directly on the element when using your device without Switch Control enabled.

Disable Switch Control by triple tapping the home button or sleep button on your device to activate the Accessibility Shortcut, then double tap the screen once Switch Control is highlighted.

Voice Control

Voice Control is a new feature for iOS 13 and allows full control of your app using only voice, making it ideal for people with the most limited of movement. Voice Control uses the same accessibility user interface as VoiceOver, Switch Control, and different assistive technologies, meaning

your app supports it by default. As with the other assistive technologies.
your accessible user interface as determined from UIKit may not always be
ideal, or indeed accurate, so may require some customization.

Voice Control can be enabled with the accessibility shortcut. But
the most straightforward way to activate it may be to say "Hey Siri,
turn on Voice Control," to disable you can simply say "Turn off Voice
Control" followed by "Tap execute" to confirm. Navigating is generally
uncomplicated, as the most common command you will use is "tap"
followed by the label of the button. If you're unsure of the button's label,
say "show names" (Figure 9-7) to present bubbles with the accessibility
labels for each control.

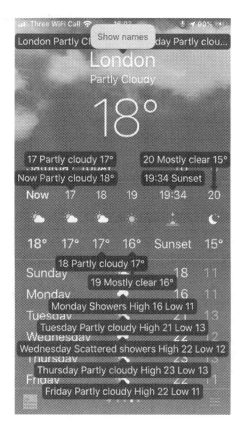

Figure 9-7. *Voice Control displaying names*

Ensure your accessibility labels for controls are accurate and brief, as this will be the phrase used by your Voice Control customers to activate the control in question. Using the "show names" command will make it evident if your labels are too long, where you have missed labels, or where labels are not easily discernible from an image.

If your element contains a large amount of content or content that is not easy for your user to speak, then, in general, this should be provided as the accessibilityValue, not the accessibilityLabel. You can also offer a group of shorter, or alternative labels that your user may speak, by providing an array of strings to your elements accessibilityUserInputLabels property (Listing 9-5), making sure to give the default label first.

Listing 9-5. Providing friendly labels for Voice Control to listen for to activate a "play" control

```
playButton?.accessibilityUserInputLabels = ["Play", "Play song",
"Play \(song.title)"]
```

Summary

- Ensuring your accessible user interface is accurate will ensure both Switch Control and Voice Control work as your customers will expect.

- If your app makes use of touch gestures, make sure you offer an alternative that doesn't require gestures. Additionally, add these as accessibility actions in your accessible user interface.

- Voice Control is a great tool to determine quickly and visually if your accessible user interface is logical. And it's fun to use.

The next chapter is the conclusion of our look at iOS' accessibility features. We'll cover the considerations iOS provides for people with hearing impairments.

CHAPTER 10

iOS Accessibility Features – Hearing

If I were to offer a single piece of advice regarding improving apps for people with hearing impairments, it would be to embed captions on any video content, either through hard coding them or preferably by adding a subtitle track and using the `AVPlayer` control to play the video. If your app makes prominent use of audio, consider an alternative way to provide an engaging experience, perhaps through leveraging animation.

Hearing Devices

Some hearing aid devices are Made for iPhone certified and can be paired to your customer's device to route audio through the device or to use the Live Listen feature to route from the iPhone's microphones right to the hearing aid. If you detect hearing aids are paired, you may want to offer the option for your customer to pan all audio to the side they are wearing a hearing aid.

If required, you can determine hearing aid paired status by registering for `hearingDevicePairedEarDidChangeNotifications` or by checking if the `hearingDevicePairedEar` option set contains either `.left`, `.right`, or `.both` (Listing 10-1).

© Rob Whitaker 2020
R. Whitaker, *Developing Inclusive Mobile Apps*,
https://doi.org/10.1007/978-1-4842-5814-9_10

Listing 10-1. Detecting changes with paired hearing devices

```swift
import UIKit

class MyViewController: UIViewController {

    var hearingDeviceStatus: UIAccessibility.HearingDeviceEar {
        get{
            return UIAccessibility.hearingDevicePairedEar
        }
    }

    override func viewDidLoad() {
        super.viewDidLoad()

        NotificationCenter.default.addObserver(self,
        selector: #selector(hearingDevicesChanged),
        name: UIAccessibility.hearingDevicePairedEarDidChange
        Notification, object: nil)
    }

    @objc
    func hearingDevicesChanged() {
        if hearingDeviceStatus.contains(.left) {
            // left ear device paired
        }
        if hearingDeviceStatus.contains(.right) {
            // right ear device paired
        }
        if hearingDeviceStatus.contains(.both) {
            // both ear devices paired
        }
```

```
        if hearingDeviceStatus.isEmpty {
            // no hearing devices paired
        }
    }
}
```

Mono Audio

Mono Audio disables stereo for all audio on the device. This is done at a system level and requires no changes by your app. Mono Audio may be used for people who have hearing loss on one side, as stereo audio can cause them to lose content if some audio is panned to the side they struggle to hear with. For instance, if a video of a conversation is panned so that one person is left and the other right, someone with hearing loss on one side will only hear half the conversation.

You might want to know about this setting if you rely on stereo audio within your app. For example, a game that might use panned audio to hint at the presence of enemies will lose meaning with this setting enabled.

monoAudioStatusDidChangeNotification will tell you when this setting is changed, and isMonoAudioEnabled will return the current status (Listing 10-2).

Listing 10-2. Detecting Mono Audio status

```
import UIKit

class MyViewController: UIViewController {

    var monoAudioStatus: Bool {
        get{
            return UIAccessibility.isMonoAudioEnabled
        }
    }
```

```
override func viewDidLoad() {
    super.viewDidLoad()

    NotificationCenter.default.addObserver(self, selector:
    #selector(monoAudioChanged), name: UIAccessibility.
    monoAudioStatusDidChangeNotification, object: nil)
}

@objc
func monoAudioChanged() {
  // check monoAudioStatus for current status.
  // provide alternatives if your app uses stereo audio.
  }
}
```

Subtitles and Captioning

Audio description can be enabled in the Accessibility settings for the device. AVFoundation contains built-in support for both audio descriptions and closed captioning, so using an AVPlayer instance for your media will give you this functionality for free (Figure 10-1) – providing you ensure your videos have audio description and closed captions embedded.

Figure 10-1. *AVPlayer displaying embedded captions*

What if you're not playing video with AVPlayer? Maybe you're using a different control, perhaps you want to display captions as part of your UI, or possibly you have a speech audio track played in your app. In these circumstances, you need to show the captions yourself. Bear in mind with this option that you will not only be responsible for displaying the captions, but you'll also need to keep the captions in sync with the audio. To decide if you should show or hide captions, you can listen to isClosedCaptioningEnabled to determine whether to display captions and closedCaptioningStatusDidChangeNotification will report any changes (Listing 10-3). Arguably, for video that is a part of UI as opposed to content, showing captions by default is always a better option.

Listing 10-3. Detecting changes in caption status

```
import UIKit

class MyViewController: UIViewController {

    var captionsStatus: Bool {
        get{
            return UIAccessibility.isClosedCaptioningEnabled
        }
    }

    override func viewDidLoad() {
        super.viewDidLoad()

        NotificationCenter.default.addObserver(self,
        selector: #selector(captionsStatusChanged),
        name: UIAccessibility.closedCaptioningStatusDidChange
        Notification, object: nil)
    }

    @objc
    func captionsStatusChanged() {
```

```
    // check captionsStatus for current status.
    // hide/show captions as requested.
  }
}
```

Most professional video-editing software will allow you to add a subtitle track to your videos. Ideally, these should be professionally transcribed, but YouTube offers a good, free, auto-generated alternative as part of their YouTube Studio software.[1] If you chose to use this service, check the titles are accurate, and edit anything YouTube has guessed wrong. You can then download the subtitles you've generated, and import them into your video editor.

As VoiceOver detects text on the screen, it can also be used as an alternative way to add audio description to videos without an audio description track. By enabling subtitles for your video, with VoiceOver enabled, your captions will then be read as they appear. However, this is no real replacement for an accurate audio description track.

Summary

- If you detect a customer has a hearing accessibility feature enabled, they might struggle to determine speech or audio directionality. Consider offering alternatives if these are important to your app.

- Use your video-editing software to embed a subtitle track into any video content your app uses, and use the AVPlayer control to display captions for you.

Now that we have covered the full range of iOS accessibility features a developer might need to consider, we need to ensure our changes are having the right impact for our customers. Next we'll consider different techniques for testing your app's accessibility.

---

[1]https://support.google.com/youtube/answer/2734796?hl=en

CHAPTER 11

Testing for Accessibility

This book will give you a whole bunch of tools and practical tips you can use when creating your apps, from design, coding, and to the service as a whole. How you use this knowledge in your app must be based on your team's consideration of how it best fits for what you are trying to achieve. None of these tools will have the impact needed by real people however, unless you check your work.

Don't consider accessibility testing as an extra. As with coding, you should aim for accessibility to become a regular part of your workflow. Include considerations for accessibility testing as part of your existing testing plan. As such, I'm not going to teach you the basics of making a test strategy; instead, I will provide tips and tools that should become second nature.

Automated Testing

Several automated testing tools exist for checking your app meets an accessible standard. Including one of these into your existing continuous integration suite will help to ensure you accessibility standard is consistently high. Having an accessibility quality gate like this will also encourage developers to consider accessibility to a high standard, in the knowledge that they won't be able to ship their code if it isn't.

© Rob Whitaker 2020
R. Whitaker, *Developing Inclusive Mobile Apps*,
https://doi.org/10.1007/978-1-4842-5814-9_11

Remember, accessibility is about how your customers experience your app, not checking boxes. There are only certain things automated accessibility tests can check for. Some commercial tools have been created as regulatory compliance tools, designed to provide proof if ever required, that you have followed accessibility guidelines. This is great if your main goal is not to get sued for poor accessibility. I feel a better way to prevent accessibility-based legal disputes would be to create a more accessible app. Use these tools as a way to prevent regressions, but they're not a substitute for manual testing or user testing.

The main benefit of tools such as these is that you can integrate them into your existing CI/CD pipelines. This way, they act as a quality gate before release. Any commits that don't reach your standard for accessibility just won't get released to your customers.

Google GTXiLib

Google provides an open source automated accessibility testing tool for iOS. GTXiLib,[1] or Google Toolbox for Accessibility, fits in with XCTest UI testing frameworks such as Google's own EarlGrey.

GTXiLib ensures your elements have a suitable hit target size, have an accessibility label which is not punctuated, and doesn't end in "button" if it's a button. There are checks for conflicting accessibility traits and contrast between labels and their background. The contrast check only works with labels, not other elements I would expect such as buttons.

Deque WorldSpace Attest

Deque offers a range of services for digital accessibility, such as training and assessment. Their web site also features a big selection of blogs and resources on digital accessibility.

---

[1]https://github.com/google/GTXiLib

Deque's WorldSpace Attest[2] product is an accessibility testing toolkit for iOS, Android, and the Web. For mobile, this works by including a framework into your app. You can then integrate tests into existing unit test suites on either Android or iOS. Instantiate a view, then pass it to the Attest function to produce test failures where accessibility issues occur.

Tests include checking for dynamically resizable text, button size, text elements presented outside scroll views, and overlapping controls.

XCUI Testing

iOS' first-party UI testing framework, XCUI, performs its tests by checking against your app's accessibility tree. This means any well-written XCUI test is also an accessibility test. It also means an accessible app is one that is easier to write automated tests for.

Finding elements by their label in XCUITests is a must (Listing 11-1). The alternatives, such as finding elements by accessibility identifier, while they do guarantee there is an element on screen, don't ensure you have set content to it or that your content is correct. If you can't find an element, this may be because you have set the element hidden to accessibility. At the same time, don't be tempted to make elements available to accessibility for the sake of testing as this would provide a bad experience for your users.

Listing 11-1. Finding a button element from its label "My Button"

```
let myButton = XCUIApplication().buttons["My Button"]
```

Once you have an element, it is then possible to perform some accessibility sanity checks on it. These checks could take the form of asserting buttons are capitalized and don't end in a period or that interactive elements are a minimum of 44px x 44px (Listing 11-2). I have

---

[2]www.deque.com/tools/worldspace-attest/

included some example tests you could use below (Listing 11-2 and Listing 11-3). Further tests I have made available are in a library called A11yUITests[3] that you can pull in as a dependency of your XCUITests.

Listing 11-2. Checking all buttons on screen have a large enough tap target

```
import XCTest

class AccessibilityTests: XCTestCase {

    let app = XCUIApplication()

    override func setUp() {
      app.launch()
    }

    func test_buttonAllButtons() {
        // Navigate to the screen you want to check

        let buttons = app.buttons.allElementsBoundByIndex

        for button in buttons {
           check(button: button)
        }
    }

    func check(button: XCUIElement) {
        XCTAssert(button.frame.size.height >= 44)
        XCTAssert(button.frame.size.width >= 44)
        XCTAssertTrue(button.label.count <= 40)
        XCTAssert(button.label.first!.isUppercase
    }
}
```

---

[3]https://github.com/rwapp/A11yUITests

Listing 11-3. Checking image's accessibility label doesn't contain the word "image"

```swift
import XCTest

class AccessibilityTests: XCTestCase {

    let app = XCUIApplication()

    override func setUp() {
        app.launch()
    }

    func test_imageName() {
    // Navigate to the screen you want to check

        let images = app.images.allElementsBoundByIndex

        for image in images {

            XCTAssertFalse(image.label.contains("image"))
        }
    }
}
```

Espresso Testing

Android's Espresso testing framework includes a class of accessibility checks. Include these tests by importing AccessibilityChecks, and enable them with the code in Listing 11-4.

Listing 11-4. Enabling accessibility tests in Espresso

```
import androidx.test.espresso.contrib.AccessibilityChecks

@RunWith(AndroidJUnit4::class)
@LargeTest
class MyWelcomeWorkflowIntegrationTest {
    companion object {
        @Before @JvmStatic
        fun enableAccessibilityChecks() {
            AccessibilityChecks.enable()
        }
    }
}
```

Tests will then automatically execute on a view and its descendants each time an action is performed on that view. Alternatively, you can instruct Espresso to run the suite of tests on the root view, by adding `setRu nChecksFromRootView(true)`after the `enable()` call.

`AccessibilityChecks` contains tests for many common accessibility issues, such as redundant labels, accessibility label presence, and tap target size. It is also capable of checking accessibility issues other tools can't, such as traversal order and image contrast.

Verification Tools

Accessibility verification tools are a middle ground between automated testing and manual testing. They can provide a little more detail than automated testing in some areas but do require manual work to run the checks.

Google GSCXScanner

GSCX,[4] or Google Scanner for Accessibility, is a library on top of Google's GTXiLib for iOS. You can include GSCX in your internal testing apps. Here it overlays a "Perform Scan" button on your apps screen. On pressing this button, GSCX highlights any offending elements. Tapping on these highlights provides a list of failure reasons and an explanation. As GSCX uses GTXiLib under the hood, it has the same suite of checks.

If you're using GTXiLib for automated testing, this is a friendly little extra that can aid accessible development.

Deque WorldSpace Attest

If you've purchased a license for Deque's testing tool on iOS or Android, this also comes with a manual mode. Manual checks happen by navigating your app with the Attest companion application attached. The attached application can then take a snapshot of your app's accessibility tree and provide you with a detailed report of any issues found, highlighting on a screenshot where the failure occurs.

Apple Accessibility Inspector

Accessibility Inspector is part of Xcode's suite of tools. You can launch it from within Xcode from the Xcode menu ➤ Open Developer Tool. You can then run the Accessibility Inspector against your app on a device or on the simulator in one of two modes.

Quicklook allows you to target a user interface element in the simulator to view the element's accessibility properties such as label, traits, and hint (Figure 11-1). The top of the Quicklook view will give you the string that VoiceOver reads when it encounters the element. Pressing the speaker button next to this will make VoiceOver read the string.

---

[4]https://github.com/google/GSCXScanner

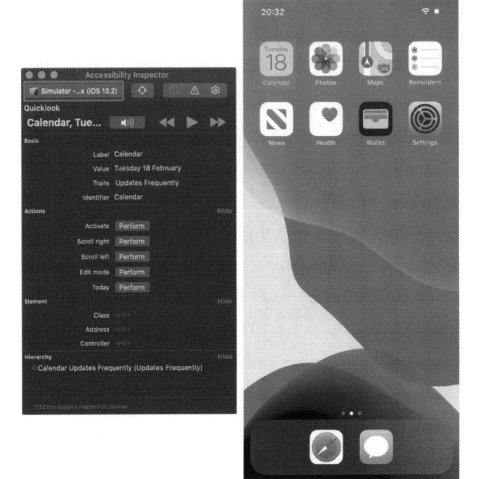

Figure 11-1. *Accessibility Inspector in Quicklook mode (left) displaying the accessibility attributes of iOS's Calendar icon, highlighted (right)*

The large Play button here will cycle through each accessible element on the screen. Accessibility Inspector does this the order VoiceOver would navigate your screen. Accessibility Inspector will read the element to you, precisely as VoiceOver will. This makes for a much faster validation technique than using VoiceOver itself.

Audit mode runs a check on the whole of the current view and reports any accessibility issues found (Figure 11-2). Reports include a more detailed description of why the verification failed, a screenshot of the element that failed in position, and a hint on how you might fix the failure. Tests include contrast, dynamic text, tap target size, and descriptions for large images.

Figure 11-2. *Accessibility inspector reporting in audit mode (left). The audit creates screenshots highlighting the area of the screen where there may be an issue (right)*

Accessibility Inspector also provides quick access to toggle some accessibility features using the Settings tab (Figure 11-3). Here you can adjust the dynamic text size. You can also toggle Invert Colors, Increase Contrast, Reduce Transparency, and Reduce Motion.

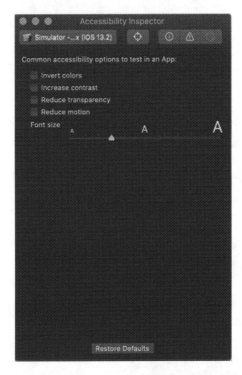

Figure 11-3. *Accessibility Inspector Settings tab providing controls for some accessibility features*

Xcode Environmental Overrides

Xcode features an Environmental Overrides menu for the currently running app. This works in both the simulator and on a device. You can find the button for this on the debugger toolbar at the bottom of your editor (Figure 11-4). Here you can effortlessly switch between dark and light modes and adjust the dynamic type size. You can also toggle several accessibility features: Increase Contrast, Reduce Transparency, Bold Text, Reduce Motion, On/Off Labels, Button Shapes, Grayscale, Smart Invert, and Differentiate Without Color.

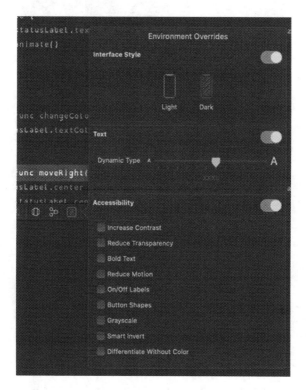

Figure 11-4. *Xcode Environmental Overrides*

Xcode Application Language

Xcode also provides overrides for testing your app in different languages, including pseudolanguages. Edit your app's build scheme by clicking the app name in the top left corner of Xcode (Figure 11-5). Under Run and Options, you'll find a dropdown option for Application Language. Here you can choose from any language supported by iOS to check your localizations. The bottom of the list also offers various pseudolanguage options (Figure 11-6).

Figure 11-5. *Editing a target's scheme in Xcode*

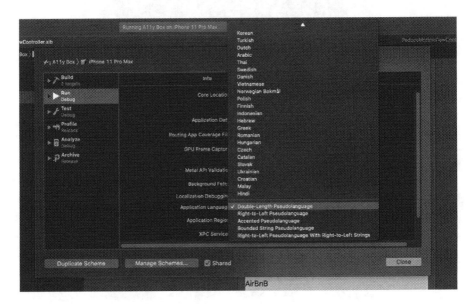

Figure 11-6. *Selecting a pseudolanguage in Xcode's scheme editor*

Pseudolanguages are synthesized languages that mimic languages with different properties. The most useful in this list are Right-to-Left Pseudolanguage and Double-Length Pseudolanguage (Figure 11-7). Right-to-Left Pseudolanguage mimics how your app will appear in a language such as Arabic that reads from the opposite direction to most languages. Double-Length Pseudolanguage duplicates your strings. This allows you to check your layout is flexible enough to support languages that take up extra room than your development language. Providing adequate flexibility in your layout will also assist your support for dynamic text sizes.

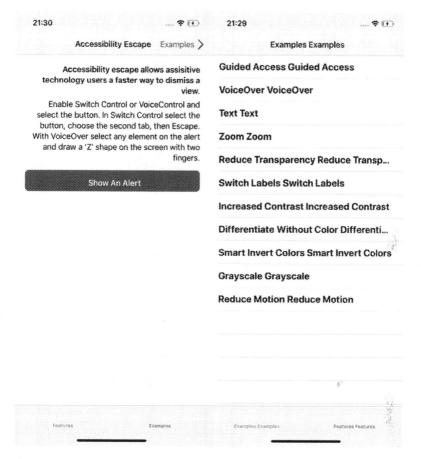

Figure 11-7. *Right-to-Left Pseudolanguage (left) and Double-Length Pseudolanguage (right)*

Google Accessibility Scanner

Google's Accessibility Scanner is an app, downloadable for free from the Google Play Store.[5] The Accessibility Scanner will run an audit against your app when requested, capturing a screenshot and highlighting elements

---

[5]https://play.google.com/store/apps/details?id=com.google.android.
apps.accessibility.auditor

that would benefit from improvements (Figure 11-8). The report provides you with the identifier of the view that has failed, along with a description of why the element failed and how you might fix the error.

Figure 11-8. *Google Accessibility Scanner making a suggestion for improving the accessibility*

Manual Testing

While automated tools and inspectors are fantastic at preventing regressions and highlighting less obvious accessibility errors, there are accessibility issues automated testing can never identify. The most common of these is determining if the accessibility tree you are presenting to your customer is logical and meaningful. While in our visual user interface, we have designers to do this for us, their hard work doesn't always translate to a useful accessibility tree once we have turned the designs into code. The only way to check this is to try it for yourself.

Screen Reader Testing

When making a new screen, or making a significant change to a screen, navigate your screen with VoiceOver or TalkBack enabled. While these screen readers make up just one assistive technology, as they all use the same accessibility tree, the experience should be comparable.

Once you become familiar with how these screen readers work, this test should become a quick and essential part of your regular development workflow. As you become more comfortable with this test, try enabling Dark Screen or Screen Curtain. These features turn off the display, meaning your only interaction with the device is through gestures and device-spoken feedback. How simple is it for you to follow your app with no visual hints at all?

What to Look Out For

When performing manual testing with screen readers, there are a few questions to ask as you're navigating.

1. **Is each element presented in a logical order?**
   Elements should follow each other in a meaningful way that provides context to controls. Don't present a "buy" button before the name of the item that's being purchased, for example.

2. **Are any elements missing?**
   It is possible for elements to be hidden to assistive technologies but still visible on the screen. Are all the content and controls on this screen read when I swipe through?

3. **Are there elements presented that I am not expecting to be present?**
   If you have hidden elements on a screen, depending on how you have hidden them, they may still be available to assistive technologies. This could result in you presenting incorrect information to your customer or allowing your customer to navigate into an invalid state.

4. **Is navigating this screen laborious?**
   Do you have to swipe between elements often? Are elements or controls repeated? Is information duplicated, like giving a button the name "button" and setting a "button" trait? Perhaps some elements could be hidden from accessibility for improved navigation without losing meaning. Consider using semantic views.

Voice Control Testing

iOS 13's new Voice Control feature is first and foremost an accessibility feature, designed for people who struggle to tap the screen. But it also hides a second very worthwhile function, as a speedy accessibility testing tool.

Enable Voice Control by saying "Hey Siri, enable Voice Control." Once enabled, say "Show numbers." iOS will display numbered bubbles next to each interactive element (Figure 11-9). This number represents the tab order that VoiceOver will access each element in. A quick glance at these numbers will confirm if you are missing elements or have elements you weren't expecting to appear. It will also help you verify the order of each element makes sense within the context of the screen.

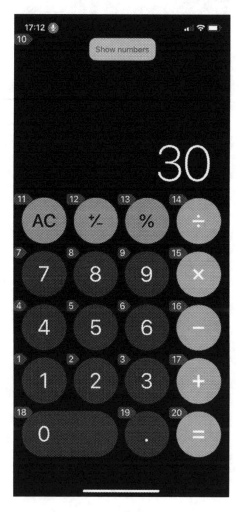

Figure 11-9. *Voice Control displaying accessibility tab order*

Next, say "Show names." iOS will replace these numbered bubbles with named bubbles featuring the accessibility label of each interactive element (Figure 11-10). This allows you to validate the labels exist and are meaningful.

Figure 11-10. Voice Control displaying accessibility labels

User Feedback

Consider adding an option in your app for your customers to contact you with feedback. AppleVis, an online community of blind and low-vision Apple users, recommends its members contact app developers when they have experienced accessibility issues to outline the problem.[6] Many people who discover accessibility concerns do just that. The reality is that many developers don't know enough about accessibility to know there could be an issue. People who do email feedback tend to find they get good results from this. But even if you're following everything in this book, you still won't have the experience your customers do when using your app. A feedback option is a low-cost, low-effort but effective way of doing user testing.

One benefit we have as mobile developers, although it's perhaps not always a benefit, is that we receive feedback from our customers in the form of app reviews. Look at these regularly, and identify trends. Look out for people complaining about a lack of a feature that does appear in your app. This is not the fault of your users for not finding this; your feature is either not intuitive or not discoverable enough.

User Testing

Earlier in this book, I emphasized the importance of having empathy in software engineering. Empathy is an incredibly valuable skill for any software craftsperson. But empathy can sometimes lead us down the wrong path – the path toward thinking something must be done but not thinking about whether what we chose to do is having the effect we are looking for. One reason for improving accessibility in your app indeed is because helping others makes you feel good, but that shouldn't be the main reason. Design strategist Liz Jackson asks us to rethink the strategy of empathy.

---

[6]https://applevis.com/apps

[Empathy] reifies class and power structures. You always have the empathizer and then you always have the empathizee, right? The empathizer is cast as the saviour, and the empathizee is always the recipient and those roles never change. [Empathy] silences the recipient. You are expected to be grateful for that which has been done for you.

—Liz Jackson, Empathy Reifies Disability Stigmas[7]

Accessibility consultant and sign language user Marie van Driessche tells us that from her experience, empathy is used as an excuse for not talking to people with disabilities.

Most people are not interested in talking to disabled people, they prefer to empathize. But empathy is not helping us.

—Marie van Driessche[8]

My point here is that if you're not user testing your app with users with disabilities, you're not doing accessibility. You're merely wasting your development time by boosting your ego.

There are many books dedicated to user testing that will cover how to do this with far more expertise than I can, so I won't cover how to set up user testing sessions or labs. But I do wish to express how important it is to make your participants in user testing sessions varied. Be sure to include people with disabilities, along with people from different backgrounds, and various technical abilities. Most importantly, listen to their feedback.

---

[7]Jackson, Liz. "Empathy Reifies Disability Stigmas" https://vimeo.com/319388683

[8]Van Driessche, Marie. Twitter post. September 4th, 2019. https://twitter.com/marievandries/status/1169242121108369409

It may be the case that a change you made thinking it would improve accessibility has made it worse. Disabled people don't have an obligation to be grateful to you for considering them. Instead, your duty as a developer is to work with their feedback.

Summary

- As with any other aspect of software, if you don't test it, how do you know it worked?

- The most accurate and useful form of accessibility testing is user testing with people with a range of (dis) abilities. Be sure to listen to and trust their experiences.

- User testing can be time-consuming and expensive, so consider including automated testing as part of your standard release process. However, you shouldn't rely too heavily on automated testing as they are limited in scope.

CHAPTER 12

Making Your App Inclusive

By now, I'm hoping I've convinced you on the argument of why accessibility and inclusion are essential. And we've covered what each platform is capable of and why. But when and how should you use each of the tools Google and Apple have created for you? In this chapter, we'll discuss some of the techniques you can use to improve your app's experience for different people. In no specific order, we'll cover different groups of people and discuss some of the ways you can make your app more inclusive. We'll combine elements of graphic design, service design, and mobile programming.

The ultimate aim is to make our apps a truly inclusive experience. As you read through, you'll likely notice some themes appear. This is no accident. To aim to fix your app for one group of people is not inclusive but exclusive. By sticking to principles of around design, flexibility, and respect for our customer, we can create software that works better for everyone.

Dyslexia, Autism, and Learning Difficulties

People who fit into this category, along with people with other disorders such as ADHD, bipolar disorder, and others, are often known as neurodiverse. I like the framing this word provides; it shifts away from the

© Rob Whitaker 2020
R. Whitaker, *Developing Inclusive Mobile Apps*,
https://doi.org/10.1007/978-1-4842-5814-9_12

idea that neurodiverse people have something to be overcome. People who consider themselves neurodiverse feel that their brain works in a way different to the rest of us. I am dyslexic, and while this does cause me issues, namely, reading and math, I feel the difference in how my brain processes information provides me with unique perspectives. It has taken me many years, and I'll always be learning something new, but I feel I have a grasp on how I can use these differences as an advantage. There are a few things you can do to make your app's experience for neurodiverse people, including me, a happier one.

Design Simplicity

Sticking to sound design principles will have a significant impact on many people with learning difficulties. Keep your design consistent, simple, clean, and uncluttered. Stick to platform norms for added consistency.

Any moving or animating content must include a mechanism for your customer to pause the animation, including video, but not transitions. Moving content should only ever trigger as a response to a user action.

Typography

Don't use too many fonts, text sizes, or colors. Having too much variation will make your app look messy and inconsistent. But for some people with learning difficulties, too many differences can make reading harder. Avoid bold, underline, italic, and all caps text.

For body text, use black text on a light colored, but not white, background. If possible, allowing users to select a background color is ideal. Body text should always be naturally justified (left in most languages). If your design calls for center- or right-justified text, this is OK, but avoid fully justified text as this creates a wall of text that can be hard to decipher.

Clear Written Content

Keep written content concise and descriptive. Be explicit about the consequence of any action. Use these same principles for buttons and other controls. Avoid the use of idioms, acronyms, and abbreviations as these can be difficult to comprehend.

The Plain English Campaign provides free advice on their web site[1] for writing clear English in a way that will get your message across and still be an engaging read. Hemmingway (`www.hemingwayapp.com`, seen in Figure 12-1) is a great free web app that will check your grammar and provide your text with a US school reading grade, highlighting areas for improvement.

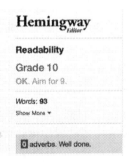

Figure 12-1. *Hemmingway highlighting areas I can improve my writing for readability. Most of this book featured less red highlighting than this paragraph, honest*

Alternatives to Text

Don't present solely text-based information. Provide redundancy in the form of an image, graph, or video. For larger groups of text, or for text that you can't easily convert into a visual form, provide an audio recording.

---

[1]"How to write in plain English", The Plain English Campaign. `http://www.plainenglish.co.uk/how-to-write-in-plain-english.html`. Accessed 20th November 2019.

Both iOS and Android provide screen readers – Select to Speak on Android and Speak Selection and Speak Screen on iOS. Note that these are not the same as VoiceOver and Talk Back. VoiceOver and TalkBack include a navigation element and are designed for users with visual impairments. Screen readers read only text content. They don't read or facilitate interaction with controls. You should test your app with the screen reader enabled to ensure it reads your content in a meaningful and understandable way. You may need to change your app's accessibility tree to give the best experience.

Color

For some people with learning difficulties, specific color combinations can make text appear jumbled or to strobe. Avoid bright, vivid color, especially around content. Use black for text rather than a shade of gray or color, regardless of how close to black that color may be. The background for text content should be a pale color; pastel colors work well. Avoid white or other bright colors. Ideally, allow your customer to choose a background color that suits them.

Accuracy

Don't insist on accuracy for written input. Instead, provide options. With limited options, allow your customer to select from a spinner or by pressing a button. Where options are broader, such as a text box, provide the opportunity for auto-completion or suggestions to reduce the amount of typing. As much as possible, try to ensure these suggestions don't need perfect spelling to appear.

For longer passages, allow entering text by dictation. Dictation is supported by default on both platforms but can be disabled if your app is providing its own keyboard, so prefer the system keyboard where possible.

Enable autocorrection for any standard text entry. Always allow the opportunity for your user to review and edit any content they have entered before they commit to submitting.

Full Disclosure

User experience specialist Harry Brignull coined the phrase dark patterns in 2010 to identify hostile design patterns intended to make users do things they hadn't intended to. Harry defined some common dark patterns on his web site, darkpatterns.org.[2] These include, but are not limited to, trick questions, confirm shaming, and misdirection. 2019 research from Cornell University identified a total of 15 different types of dark pattern across popular online shopping web sites. The researchers found over 11% of the highest ranked commerce sites featuring at least one example.[3] Let's be clear on this: dark patterns intended to trick your user show contempt for all your users and are always unethical. For your customers with learning difficulties, these traps are even more upsetting and confusing.

Be clear about the consequences of performing an action, and don't then change consequences later without explicit consent. If you're collecting phone numbers for 2FA, for example, don't then use this to start sending SMS spam. The sudden arrival of unexpected messages for an unknown reason could be worrying.

---

[2]"Types of Dark Pattern", Dark Patterns. `https://www.darkpatterns.org/types-of-dark-pattern`. Accessed November 20, 2019.

[3]Mathur, Arunesh et al. "Dark Patterns at Scale." Proceedings of the ACM on Human-Computer Interaction 3.CSCW (2019). `https://arxiv.org/pdf/1907.07032.pdf`.

Anxiety and Mental Health

Many headlines are covering the health effects of smartphones: "Putting Down Your Phone May Help You Live Longer,"[4] endless opinion pieces such as "How I Ditched My Phone and Unbroke My Brain,[5] and a wealth of health guides like "5 ways your phone is affecting your anxiety."[6] Seeing these headlines, it may be tempting to believe we mobile devs have created a monster.

Panics about information overload and new technologies are older than technology itself. In around 360 BC, Socrates warned the written word would "create forgetfulness" and that readers would struggle to differentiate fantasy from reality.[7] It is true that Internet or mobile phone addiction exists and that it can be as damaging as any other addiction. It's also true that overuse of smartphones can cause stress, depression, sleeping problems, anxiety, and loneliness.[8]

While overuse of technology is an indicator of poor mental health, so is technology underuse. Bélanger and colleagues in a 2010 study found a

---

[4]Price, Catherine. "Putting Down Your Phone May Help You Live Longer". The New York Times, April 24, 2019. `www.nytimes.com/2019/04/24/well/mind/putting-down-your-phone-may-help-you-live-longer.html`.

[5]Roose, Kevin, "Do Not Disturb: How I Ditched My Phone and Unbroke My Brain". The New York Times, February 23, 2019. `https://www.nytimes.com/2019/02/23/business/cell-phone-addiction.html`

[6]Jones, Eleanor, "5 ways your phone is affecting your anxiety". Cosmopolitan, February 14, 2018. `www.cosmopolitan.com/uk/body/health/a17851630/mobile-phone-affecting-anxiety-mental-health/`

[7]Plato, "Phaedrus". Athens, 360BCE. `http://classics.mit.edu/Plato/phaedrus.html`

[8]Noë, Beryl et al. "Identifying Indicators of Smartphone Addiction Through User-App Interaction". Computers in Human Behavior, Vol 99. October 2019, pp 56-65. `www.sciencedirect.com/science/article/pii/S0747563219301712`

"U-shaped association" between Internet use and mental health.[9] Their oft-cited research discovered that those with little or no Internet use had increased levels of depression resulting from feeling isolated. So, while our chosen platform may cause the effects listed above for some, for the majority, it has the exact opposite effect. By creating immersive experiences, we allow people to enrich their lives and find belonging. This is something we should celebrate.

Determining what areas of smartphone use are risk factors for mental health is all but impossible. The wide range of tasks that we can perform on smartphones, combined with the fact that heavy smartphone use is a societal norm, make it very difficult to identify patterns.[10] But we can apply some more general research into mental health risk factors to create some guidelines.

Guide

The feeling of being lost or trapped can be catalysts for anxiety. A common occurrence of this in mobile is forcing your customer to perform actions at a time chosen by us, for example, showing an interstitial, rather than allowing our customer to make the decision when they're ready. Attempting to make our users choose our preferred outcome by hiding alternative options is another pattern I see all too often.

You can combat feelings of disorientation by guiding and signposting. Display your customer's progress to them when they are performing a

---

[9]Bélanger, Richard E. et al. "A U-Shaped Association Between Intensity of Internet Use and Adolescent Health". Pediatrics, vol. 127, no 2. February 2011. https://pediatrics.aappublications.org/content/127/2/e330

[10]Noë, "Identifying Indicators of Smartphone Addiction Through User-App Interaction"

task to reiterate what they have achieved and how much they have left.[11] Allow your customer to progress at their own pace. And, if possible, allow your customer to advance in their order, skipping, or returning to steps as necessary.

When your customer has completed a task, before they commit, offer the opportunity to check what they've done. Allow the chance to change their responses as necessary. If any action is going to make a noticeable change in service, such as a destructive action, explain the consequences in an easy-to-follow manner before allowing your customer to commit. We often have the aim of speeding up our customer's interactions within our app, but consider employing positive friction if your flow could result in a significant change or a negative outcome. Positive friction provides a pause allowing your customer chance to double check their actions.[12]

Make sure your app's look and feel are consistent, sticking with system controls where possible to aid consistency with the platform. Changes in the way something works, especially unexpected ones, can cause feelings of discomfort and increase anxiety.

Communicate

Visibility is vital for anxiety, and communicating clearly and timely to your customer has a positive effect.[13] Investing in a good copywriter will provide a significant benefit to the clarity of your app. Intelligible, concise communication about the consequences of actions before your user has

---

[11]"Highlight Where People Are", Design Patterns for Mental Health. Accessed November 20, 2019. www.designpatternsformentalhealth.org/pattern-library/highlight-where-people-are

[12]"Monzo: Designing good mental health into the way we bank", Design Council. Accessed 20 November 2019. www.designcouncil.org.uk/news-opinion/monzo-designing-good-mental-health-way-we-bank

[13]"Monzo: Designing good mental health into the way we bank", Design Council.

made them is essential. If you are making changes to a service, such as a redesign, be sure to communicate these in advance.[14]

If your app features paid services in the form of in-app purchases or subscriptions, don't hide any costs. Make any options for paid services transparent upfront, and make it explicit what the services do and don't include. Allow your customers to cancel at any time, without jumping through hoops. As with informing your customer before they begin a paid service, make sure you're clear about what they will lose if they cancel. An option to pause a paid service is a great addition.[15]

Aim to do all this while keeping in mind not to bombard your customer with information. Provide them with clear, easy-to-understand relevant information, but keep it short and quick to read at a glance. If your customer needs more information, direct them to where they can access it. Ideally, provide support with a real person. Set expectations about what support can offer, when it's available, and how long it will take to respond.[16]

Self-control

Many people with anxiety, mental disorders, or learning difficulties will often find the ability to add restrictions on themselves a positive action. A 2019 study from Noë and colleagues found that apps that don't provide a defined endpoint to content, for example, infinite scrolling, can lead

---

[14]"Positive Update", Design Patterns for Mental Health. Accessed 20 November 2019. www.designpatternsformentalhealth.org/pattern-library/positive-update

[15]"No Strings Attached", Design Patterns for Mental Health. Accessed 20th November 2019. www.designpatternsformentalhealth.org/pattern-library/no-strings-attached

[16]"Immediate Support", Design Patterns for Mental Health. Accessed 20th November 2019. www.designpatternsformentalhealth.org/pattern-library/immediate-support

to smartphone addiction.[17] Forcing a stop to our smartphone use allows us to take a break and refocus. Implementing these controls in your app will vary greatly depending on your app's purpose. I have included some examples here for inspiration.

A great example of allowing customers to manage themselves comes from UK Challenger bank Monzo. Monzo put in place blocks on certain transactions in their app, providing a setting for customers to disallow any transactions related to online gambling. Apple has also implemented some self-control features into iOS with Screen Time (Figure 12-2 and Figure 12-3). This feature allows us to add a limit to how much time we can spend in certain apps, categories, or on the phone as a whole. We can also set a downtime when we only want certain essential apps to be available.

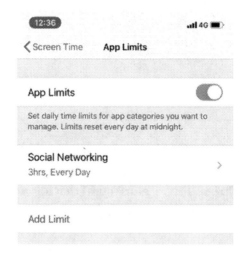

Figure 12-2. *Setting a limit to social media use with iOS' Screen Time feature*

---

[17]Noë, "Identifying Indicators of Smartphone Addiction Through User-App Interaction"

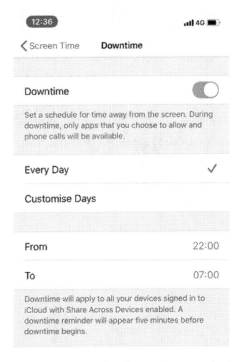

Figure 12-3. *Setting an overnight downtime period with iOS' Screen Time feature*

Social Interaction

Digital services are an invaluable tool for allowing people to become social and find belonging. Adding a social aspect to your app can be a great way for like-minded people to discover each other and greatly benefit their mental well-being.

But as we cover in the section on Gender and Sexuality below, any way users can interact with each other can also be just as much of a detriment, to both your customer's well-being and your business. It's essential to prove a mechanism for customers to block content and users, and preferably a moderation system, for any form of interaction between your users.

Gamification

At its best, gamification is the digital experiences fork of nudge theory. Nudge theory is the behavioral science field that investigates using positive reinforcement to encourage positive actions. The most quoted example is that of adding images of house flies into urinals at Amsterdam's Schiphol Airport. By adding the fly in the right spot of the urinal, it was discovered that men's aim was significantly improved and spillage reduced by 80%.[18] Gamification can be used as a means of making experiences more positive and has been shown to work well in patients with severe mental illness.[19]

Duolingo (Figure 12-4), the language learning app, has used gamification to become both the most downloaded and most used learning app on the app store. It does this using a combination of small, achievable, progressive goals, visualizing progress, and prompts to return and stay engaged.[20]

---

[18]Richard H. Thaler, Cass R. Sunstein. "Nudge: Improving Decisions About Health, Wealth, and Happiness." 2009.

[19]Brownlee, John, "Designing An App For People With Severe Mental Illness." Fast Company, March 17, 2016. www.fastcompany.com/3057872/ designing-an-app-for-people-with-severe-mental-illness

[20]Draycott, Richard, "Gamification is the key to Duolingo success says product manager Gilani at Canvas conference". The Drum, October 26, 2016. www. thedrum.com/news/2017/10/26/gamification-the-key-duolingo-success-says-product-manager-gilani-canvas-conference

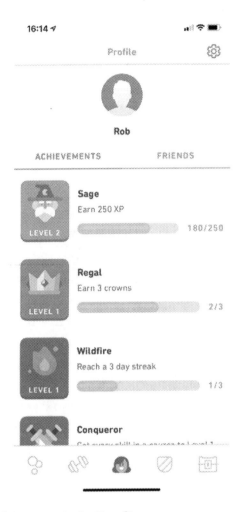

Figure 12-4. *Achievements in Duolingo*

While we can certainly criticize the increasingly needy, anxiety-inducing, push notifications Duolingo sends when you haven't been paying enough attention; Duolingo, for the most part, is an excellent example of gamification done well. It's colorful, friendly, and fun and importantly doesn't push users into paying.

Gamification is all too often a euphemism for psychological manipulation, making your users do something they otherwise wouldn't, be that spending money, performing tasks, sharing personal data or one of many other examples. Both app stores are full of "freemium" games, Candy Crush and Clash of Clans being famous examples. Many of these such games, while appearing free, require substantial real money investment to make significant progress.

UK mobile network GiffGaff has replaced some of their core business operations such as support and sales with customers, or "community members" as GiffGaff calls them. Points are earned for each task completed, like replying to a fellow customer's support query in app. GiffGaff rewards community members with lower prices for everyone. Any points earned are redeemable for credit against customer's bills. Providing rewards for positive customer behavior can be a great way of increasing customer loyalty, encouraging the practices your app needs and making your experience more enjoyable. But for me, outsourcing core business functions to your customers crosses an ethical labor boundary.

It's a subtle but important line between engaging your customers with gamification and seeding bad habits. Noë and colleagues suggest that gamification in the form of competing against friends online can be a cause of smartphone addiction.[21] Noë's team uses the example of Snapchat's Snapstreak feature. Snapstreak rewards regular posting with a fire emoji and the number of days the streak has been maintained. Users are encouraged to keep this streak alive. But this can cause users to feel pressured into posting and can result in high levels of stress and anxiety.

---

[21]Noë, "Identifying Indicators of Smartphone Addiction Through User-App Interaction."

Financially Disadvantaged

A computer, tablet, or smartphone along with an Internet connection is not an insignificant financial outlay, and a recurring one too. For an estimated 20% of Internet users, a smartphone is their only access to the Internet.[22] Smartphone-only Internet users are far more likely to live in deprived areas. 40% of them say their reason for using a smartphone because of the cost involved with other options.

We then have a responsibility as mobile developers to ensure we maintain feature parity with desktop experiences. There is a delicate balance to be struck too around the devices we support. Dropping support for older devices and operating systems can bring us benefits like reduced complexity and exciting new features. But the users we may be leaving without apps are commonly those who are most disadvantaged and may struggle to upgrade.

Consider too that people with disabilities often have a more substantial cost burden than those without — UK Disability charity Scope estimates this to be over $750US extra per month.[23] People with disabilities are also more likely to be out of full-time employment. The United States has an employment rate of 3.7%; this rises to 8% among people with disabilities.[24] So, people with disabilities are more likely to fall into the financially disadvantaged category.

---

[22]"Locked Out: The Smartphone Deficit", Citizens Advice Scotland. August 2018. www.cas.org.uk/publications/locked-out-smartphone-deficit

[23]John, Evan., Thomas, Greg., and Touchet, Anel. "The Disability Price Tag 2019" February 2019. www.scope.org.uk/campaigns/extra-costs/disability-price-tag/

[24]"Persons with a Disability: Labor Force Characteristics Summary" US Bureau of Labor. February 26, 2019. Statistics. www.bls.gov/news.release/disabl.nr0.htm

Digital Literacy

You're an expert. While we all have our own specialisms in software engineering, you're still an expert. There are many people for whom anything digital is a mystery, perhaps because they lack the financial means. Perhaps they grew up at a time when computers were not ubiquitous and found no reason to learn. As a regular, long-time digital citizen, it's easy to forget about, or look down on, the many people who don't use the Internet, maybe even people who are scared of the Internet. But worries about online banking, for example, are genuine and one that 80% of us share.[25]

Essential Digital Skills

The UK Government, in consultation with groups such as Amazon and Microsoft, has produced a list of Essential Digital Skills.[26] The government considers these skills to be the benchmark for any person to be able to use the Internet competently.

As you're reading this book, I'm going to guess that you can do all these essential digital skills. Indeed, many of them may seem so basic they're barely worth mentioning. The reality for many people in the United Kingdom, however, is that they can't do these things we'd consider obvious. 21% of the UK adult population, 11.3 million people, don't have these skills.[27] More concerning is that 8% of the UK adult population, 4.3 million, don't have any of these skills – not a single one. I have summarized some of the key skills and some of those most relevant to mobile.

---

[25]"Lloyds Bank UK Consumer Digital Index 2018" Lloyds Bank. May 2018. https://www.lloydsbank.com/assets/media/pdfs/banking_with_us/whats-happening/LB-Consumer-Digital-Index-2018-Report.pdf

[26]"Essential digital skills framework," Department for Education. April 23, 2019. www.gov.uk/government/publications/essential-digital-skills-framework/essential-digital-skills-framework

[27]"Lloyds Bank UK Consumer Digital Index 2018" Lloyds Bank.

Communicating

The skills required to communicate, collaborate, and share information, include skills such as

- I can set up a group on messaging platforms, such as WhatsApp or Messenger, to talk to friends or family members.

- I can post appropriately on social media and visit and post to forums such as Mumsnet or Reddit.

- I can send photographs and other documents to friends and family as an email attachment.

- I understand the importance of communicating securely.

Handling Information and Content

The skills required to find, manage, and store digital information and content securely include

- I understand that not all online information and content that I see is reliable.

- I can use search engines to find information and make use of search terms to generate better results.

- I understand that the Cloud is a way that I can store information and content in a remote location.

- I can stream music from legal sites such as Spotify or Apple Music or watch streamed movies from legal sources such as Netflix or Amazon Prime.

Transacting

The following skills are required to register and apply for services, buy and sell goods and services, and administer and manage transactions online:

- I can set up online accounts for public services.

- I can set up online accounts for government services and retailers to order and pay for goods online such as through Amazon or eBay.

- I can use travel web sites and apps to book tickets and make reservations.

- I can securely manage my money and transactions online.

Problem-Solving

The skills required to find solutions to problems using digital tools and online services:

- I can use online tutorials, FAQs, and advice forums to solve problems and improve my skills in using devices, software, and applications.

- I can find out how to do something by using a tutorial video such as those found on YouTube.

- I can use the Internet to find specific information related to life tasks that need to be carried out, for example, finding a recipe or finding information that helps plan travel.

Being Safe and Legal Online

The skills required to stay safe, legal, and confident online in both life and work include

- I keep the information I use to access my online accounts secure, using different and secure passwords for web sites and accounts, and make sure that I don't share this with anyone.

- I can recognize suspicious links in email, web sites, social media messages, and pop ups and know that clicking these links or downloading unfamiliar attachments could put me and my computer at risk.

- I understand the risks and threats involved in carrying out activities online and the importance of working securely.

- I understand why it is important to keep my computer systems and security software up to date, and I allow them to be updated when prompted.

Findings

Of the five areas outlined above, the most highly skilled area is handing information and content. 91% of the population have adequate skills in this category. Yet, 21% of respondents weren't able to download or save a photo they found online.

Despite an increasing amount of our interactions with organizations being digital, between 2015 and 2018, there has only been around a 1–2% growth in these skills. Only 87% of people were able to complete an online application form, and 85% were able to buy an item or service online. Of particular interest to us in mobile is that only 76% of people were able to install an app on their device.

You ≠ Your Users

In the past 25 years we have been designing [software] mostly for people who design [software].

—Vasilis van Gemert, Exclusive Design [28]

As people who make a living, one way or another, from computers, it's easy for us to forget that we are in a privileged position when it comes to knowing how to use the products we create. In reality, our customers are not like us; they're not even that likely to be like our friends.

I'm sure we can all think of a family member who doesn't use technology. If they needed to pick up a device today to do a task, will they know that the frying pan icon means they can search? Will they care about the cutesy names you've given to things, like "the cloud" when you mean storage? I remember a time from working in an Apple reseller. A customer believed AirPort, Apple's brand name for Wi-Fi, meant they could only use Wi-Fi on flights.

We can't be there to hold our customer's hands. And I don't think either us or our customers would want that either. There's a fine line between thinking about what our customers are capable of and being patronizing. Avoiding jargon, both written and visual, is an excellent first step. To be successful at the rest, we need to know more about our users.

User Testing

When developing any product, it's essential to know the market and who your customer base is. Why should this be any different when we're creating software? There's no reason why we, as developers, can't talk to our users. Apart from that, many of us prefer as little human interaction as possible.

---

[28]van Gemert, Vasilis, "Exclusive Design". Accessed November 20, 2019. https://exclusive-design.vasilis.nl

User testing can be time-consuming and expensive. But it can be the difference between a successful product and a failure, for any size of business. A product manager may be interested in user testing for identifying the product and its market. But as developers, we can use user testing to identify our market's skills. This is precisely where the essential digital skills come in.

The UK Government developed the essential digital skills listed earlier as a user testing tool. After inviting people to experience their software, before getting hands-on, they ask questions of their participants to determine their digital skills. The participants are then plotted on a scale (Figure 12-5), starting at 0 with never have and never will use the Internet. Moving to 4, meaning the participant can do one of the essential digital skills above. 7 means the participant can perform all the essential digital skills. Finishing at 9, where you and I would sit, meaning we're experts who make our living from digital.

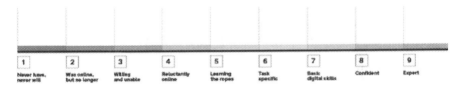

Figure 12-5. *The UK Government's digital inclusion scale*

You can use this scale in two ways. If you are genuinely confident you have an accurate cross-section of your app's user base as research participants, you can use the scale to get a read of your participants skills. The scale will help you learn how advanced and adventurous you can make your features. Just be confident that your users do follow.

Or, you can use this scale as a way to ensure your app is simple to follow. Check that, for those with lower digital skills, they can guide themselves through your app without you patronizing them.

Age

Technology has a generational gap. 99% of 11–18-year-olds have access to the Internet; 96% of them use the Internet every day. 28% of those aged over 60 are not online at all.[29] This is a vast disparity between generations. Many of us grew up with the ubiquity of computing. Others had likely never heard of computers or knew them as an obscure industrial tool they would never use. Who among us, having not grown up on a farm, would feel confident, or even enjoy, learning the intricate details of sophisticated farming machinery in our thirties if this were suddenly to become part of our everyday lives? We cover many of the issues here in a broader context in the preceding section on digital skills.

While this skills gap is gradually closing, we can't escape that the world has an aging population,[30] and with aging comes changes to our body. As life expectancy grows, it's a truism that most of us will live to see our body begin to fail us. So, although you might not use assistive technology now, in the future as your eyes, cognition, motor abilities, or any other physical facet begins to fail, you will begin to appreciate their presence. This is the same for your customers.

Text Sizes As a Gateway to Accessibility

The "gateway" accessibility feature for age is the ability to change text sizes. Supporting Dynamic Type on iOS and using scalable point sizes on Android is a must-have first step for accessibility in any app. Adjustable text sizes are commonly the first accessibility feature a customer may use, often without considering it an accessibility feature.

---

[29]"Lloyds Bank UK Consumer Digital Index 2018" Lloyds Bank.

[30]"Ageing", United Nations. Accessed November 20, 2019. www.un.org/en/sections/issues-depth/ageing/

Customizable text sizes are on the cusp between what we might think of as an accessibility feature and a customization. So, supporting these helps to normalize the use of accessibility features. It also serves to educate your user that accessibility considerations are possible on their device.

There are no specific considerations that benefit the aged over the general population. But older people are more likely to benefit from accessibility features. Ensuring you've followed the guidelines elsewhere in this book will mean your app provides a better experience for older users.

Gender and Sexuality

I remember learning about basic data types in high school. The exercise was to create a data capture form for people to register for a party. Although anyone who required registration for a party in an Excel spreadsheet would be unlikely to have very many guests. We stored age as an integer, name as a string, and gender as a Boolean. From an engineering perspective, storing gender this way has never been an excellent example for the use of Boolean values.

We should generally never represent any real-world value as a Boolean. Life very rarely is a binary choice or decision. Limiting yourself to two options is limiting the scope for future refactoring. While I have seen a person's life status represented as an enum, this is an extreme example. Although this would mean refactoring for the Night King's army of the dead less of a project once winter inevitably does come. For anything other than life and death, I'd recommend an enum, allowing future changes.

Secondly, allowing only two options for anything involving identity means making assumptions about the people who are using your app. This is true whether you make this choice actively or passively. This assumption about your customers may not be correct, and many of your users won't thank you for it.

Gender

Gender is a perfect example of why using a Boolean for real-world values is a bad idea. Gender is not, and never has been, a binary choice, but it was not too long ago that as a society, we considered it as such. Because of this societal norm, we created a lot of software to accept a binary choice of male or female.

Regardless of your personal view, there is an overriding technical software engineer perspective that tells us this was a poor choice. By programming all these systems to use an inflexible Boolean, we created a large amount of technical debt for when we inevitably change how our system works. In the example of gender identity, society is demanding that we change how the system works. This change now requires back-end database migration and front-end redesigns to allow for that expanded choice.

The software craftsperson view here is that by limiting to only two choices, we are excluding those who don't identify as male or female. We are adding to their feeling of exclusion and creating a barrier for them to take part in society. Many gender nonbinary people have been excluded by their family as teenagers or young adults and, as a result, begin life believing they don't belong. As many as 48% of nonbinary teens admit to attempting suicide.[31] Allowing people to identify themselves to our software as they identify in life is much more than a decision between data types. It is a clear sign that everyone is welcome to be who they truly are and whoever that is, they are a valued member of our society. This doesn't stop your users from identifying as male or female if that's their choice.

---

[31]Hassanein, Rokia. "New Study Reveals Shocking Rates of Attempted Suicide Among Trans Adolescents." Human Rights Campaign. September 12, 2018. www.hrc.org/blog/new-study-reveals-shocking-rates-of-attempted-suicide-among-trans-adolescen

Storing Gender

One solution to this as an engineering problem, while maintaining data validation is to store gender as an enum. As an essential minimum, I would suggest male, female, and nonbinary.

A more inclusive solution would be to present these options and more as auto-complete suggestions to a text field. We are thus allowing people to enter their own option.

Don't offer a third option of "other" or hide options behind an "other" selection. "Other" is a clear sign you're considering anyone not identifying as male or female as less important. And of course, make sure your system has an option to change gender options later.

A third, even more desirable option, is to consider why you are capturing gender at all. Unless your app covers health, I struggle to think of a genuine reason to require capturing this data.

Importantly, remember that gender $\neq$ pronouns.

Pronouns

Don't assume he/him and she/her pronouns for male and female genders, respectively. If you've followed my advice above, you won't be able to make this assumption anyway. The best option for pronouns is probably to question if you require them at all. But if your app does refer to your customers by a pronoun, make sure you provide the option separate to the option for gender. Offer a they/them option, and allow your customers to change their pronoun as they need to.

Titles

It shows basic respect for your customer to refer to them as they identify. This goes for name and pronouns too of course, but for titles, there are also other options.

Personally, I dislike being known as Mr. and would prefer to be addressed simply by my first name. Many people feel it is polite to use a title, especially in a situation where you are not friendly with the person you are addressing. Many people have rightly earned the title of Dr., Sir, Captain, etc., and not allowing these options can be disrespectful. Unfortunately, due to the now somewhat outdated class system that has generated these titles, many are gender-specific. For those that aren't gender-specific, be sure not to assume gender. Include a non-gendered Mx and probably the option for no title too.

Preferred Names

A common requirement for software is to store a legal or birth name. We expect the requirement for "real" names in software for HR, banking, or government services, for example. But it's not unusual for us to want to be known differently. My preference is to be called Rob, but my passport says Robert. This can cause me problems booking international travel through work, where the systems automatically book everything in the name Rob.

The ability to have my given name separate from my preferred name, for me, is just a convenience. I would neither have to ask colleagues to call me Rob nor correct travel bookings to match my passport. But for many, this is a crucial part of their identity. For anyone who has or is changing identity, being known by a name they no longer identify with can be hugely upsetting.

Chelsea Hostetter at the Pronoun Project observes that a "real name" policy can increase discrimination, specifically in situations where someone may be out to one group but not another.[32] Facebook's policy of flagging accounts they believe not to be using a "real" name can cause those flagged to feel like a fraud.

---

[32]Hostetter, Chelsea. "Designing for All Genders", The Pronoun Project. March 4, 2018. thepronounproject.com/blog/2018/3/4/designing-for-all-genders

Allow your customers to be known by the name that they feel comfortable with, and allow them to change this as they need to. There may be apps where a birth or legal name is required, but only collect this and use it if this is essential.

Harassment

This section could equally apply to any minority section of society and indeed any category in this book. I choose to include it here as gender and sexuality, unfortunately, provide the starkest examples of how technology can enable harassment.

Gay dating app Grindr has been used by repressive regimes to identify and, in some cases, hunt down members of the LGBTQ+ community.[33] In the United Kingdom, Grindr and other apps were used by serial killer Stephen Port to lure his victims.[34]

The reality is stark but simple. If your app provides any way for your users to interact with one another, your app can, and will, be used for harassment, regardless of your app's primary purpose. There are examples of finance apps like Square[35] and PayPal[36] being used to harass people by sending small amounts of money along with a short note. A blocking mechanism is essential anywhere personal interaction is possible. You may also need a moderation and reporting system. All of this means we need to thoroughly consider the decision to add user interaction and its consequences into our apps.

---

[33]Mccormick, Joseph. "Egyptian police use Grindr to lure gay men to hotel rooms", Pink News. October 29, 2017. www.pinknews.co.uk/2017/10/29/egyptian-police-use-grindr-to-lure-gay-men-to-hotel-rooms/

[34]"Stephen Port: Serial killer guilty of murdering four men", BBC News. November 23, 2016www.bbc.co.uk/news/uk-england-38077859

[35]Clifton, Anna Marie. Twitter post. October 22, 2016. https://twitter.com/TweetAnnaMarie/status/789957313649967104

[36]Nine. Twitter post. October 4, 2016. https://twitter.com/supernowoczesna/status/790359673702457344

Deafness and Hearing Impairments

Smartphones are predominantly a visual medium. As such, it can be easy to forget to consider hearing impairments when building apps. Especially if your app doesn't use audio, you may think hearing impairments aren't a consideration for you at all. But here are a couple of things to consider.

Clear Content

Language is complex and interconnected in the human brain. We don't, and will probably never fully appreciate how our use and understanding of language develop. This is to say, it can be a common misconception that people with deafness can compensate in other ways, for example, a high standard of literacy. This is often not the case for a couple of reasons. Losing the context of hearing language retards learning literacy skills.[37] Remember too, that spoken or written language will always be a second language for a deaf person who prefers sign language. Consequently, you should always prefer clear, concise language with a logical layout, free from idioms and sayings.

Captions

If your app uses audio in any way, you should always provide captions in one form. You can provide captions as a separately available transcript at its simplest. Ideally, embed closed captions in your videos as we covered in earlier chapters.

---

[37]Lucker, John, L. et al. "An Examination of the Evidence-Based Literacy Research in Deaf Education" American Annals of the Deaf, vol 150, no 5. 2005/2005. www.uv.es/infabra/Luckner%202005%2006%20AN%20EXAMINATION%20OF%20THE%20EVIDENCE-BASED.pdf

Remember that the same applies to audio content, not just video. If your app includes spoken voice overs, such as a game, for example, you should caption these too. Additionally, most appropriate for games, don't rely on your customer having to determine the direction from which the audio is emanating. If your game pans audio to the left to hint at a bad guy to the left, provide a visual hint too.

Physical and Motor Skills

As with every impairment we have covered, physical and motor impairments cover a wide variety of abilities. This ranges anywhere from missing a digit, thus making multi-touch gestures harder, to having minimal movement. In later life, Stephen Hawking was limited to movement through a single cheek muscle yet was famously able to operate a computer. Much like any user, your customers with physical impairments will appreciate simplicity in your user interface.

Precision

Don't insist on accuracy from your customer; all interactive elements should have a minimum size of 44 pixels in each direction. Google recommends on Android that interactive elements should be a minimum of 48 pixels. Importantly, remember to separate interactive elements too so you prevent accidental input.

Keyboard and Switch Access

Test if your application is navigable with each platform's switch access features. There are two common pitfalls to look out for.

An unfortunately common effect on the Web is the phenomenon of the "keyboard trap." Keyboard traps happen when navigating with the tab key.

It is possible to navigate to an item but not to navigate away again. I have not seen this commonly on mobile platforms, but it does happen. On mobile, this can also happen with switch control and screen readers too.

Second, ensure the logical navigation order of elements. When you read through the elements on your page without switch control enabled, did you read it in the same order the switch control feature did? An app with poor accessibility will cause keyboard highlight to jump around the screen. This random movement is frustrating at best.

Both platforms are navigable with external keyboard input, without requiring any activation by your customer. iOS does require a little help with some standard features like paging, however. The open source project KeyboardKit[38] should help with this. Where possible, implement keyboard shortcuts too.

Timeouts

People with motor issues can struggle to interact with their devices for many reasons. Using a smartphone with two steady hands will almost always be faster than anyone with any form of reduced dexterity, be that missing digits or limbs, conditions such as Parkinson's disease which causes shaking, or people with severely limited moment who use switch or voice control. Requiring customers to act within a specific time will put a significant strain on customers with motor issues.

Remove any time limits that are not essential. Where you need time limits for your customer's security or to prevent denial of service, for example, make sure these are as long as possible while maintaining security. If a time limit is due to expire, save progress and inform your customer the time limit is coming to an end. Offer them the option to extend or renew the time limit, and pick up where they left off.

---

[38]https://github.com/douglashill/KeyboardKit

Shortcuts

Wherever possible, provide shortcuts. Shortcuts could be a bypass to a common area of your app or a more straightforward way to fill out a form. As an example, if your app deals with e-commerce, you'll need a shipping and billing address for each order. Making your customer fill out both addresses in full for every order they make is an excellent way to lose any repeat customers. But for people who find interacting with your app a chore, this is more than a minor frustration. A fix here can range from letting your customer duplicate the address for both billing and shipping, through to using a postal or zip code lookup tool and for repeat customers allowing them to save addresses for later use.

Automation

For people with physical impairments, any movement can be expensive. Depending on the person's impairment, this could range from moving across a room to toggle a light switch to navigating around a smartphone screen. As such, anything that reduces the need for movement is desirable. Automation is a fantastic tool for this. Aside from automating smart homes, we can use automation to make everyday tasks within our apps and across apps touch-free.

In Android, Google provides App Actions. App Actions allow apps in specific categories to hook into the Google Assistant, which means fast access to everyday activities with a single voice command.

For iOS, Apple provides a fantastic framework for this with Siri Shortcuts. Siri intents allow your customers to not only control your app with a single voice command but also to chain activities together through the shortcuts app. Customers can then trigger shortcuts with a single tap, voice command, or even external triggers such as time, location, or tapping an NFC tag.

Visual Impairments

Adjustable text sizes and screen reader support are essential for including people with visual impairments. Supporting your customer's chosen text size is table stakes for any mobile app. If you're not listening to this setting, or if you're truncating or overlapping text at larger sizes, you need to reconsider some of your development processes. Assuming you have supported this, other sound design principles will help include those with a visual impairment of any kind.

Careful Use of Color

Color is a powerful way of quickly conveying meaning, but not everyone experiences it in the same way. Some people have deficiencies in their color perception, making differentiation difficult. Some people with blurred or impaired vision will find colors close together will blend into each other. It is vital for choosing when, where, how, and what colors to use in your app that you pick colors disparate enough that they can be easily determined. The World Wide Web Consortium's Web Content Accessibility Guidelines (Chapter 3) recommend text should have a contrast ratio of 4.5:1 against its background, or 3:1 for large text of around 18pt or larger. For higher-level compliance with WCAG, aim for a 7:1 contrast ratio.

And remember to not rely on color alone to convey meaning. While it's a great way to show status, a green or red highlight won't be visible to everyone. Remember too that different colors have different meanings across cultures. Always combine the color with shapes or text so you have a redundant way of presenting the information. Remember to add a meaningful label for TalkBack and VoiceOver.

Many online tools for checking contrast ratios exist, but I recommend downloading the free Colour Contrast Analyser (CCA) (Figure 12-6) application from The Paciello Group.[39] CCA allows you to enter colors in many formats, including hex and RGB, or you can select a color with the eyedropper tool, and tweak them with sliders. CCA will then show you an example of your chosen color combination used for both text and icons and an indication of which WCAG rules your combination passes. However, it's crucial to check your contrast works with real people, as even some passing combinations are not high enough for some. Also, the smaller the text, the higher the ratio needed.

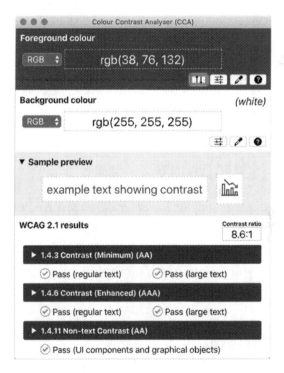

Figure 12-6. *Paciello Group's free Colour Contrast Analyser software*

---

[39]Downloadable for Mac or PC at https://developer.paciellogroup.com/resources/contrastanalyser/.

Logical Layout

A good UX design for your app will make a big difference for people with visual impairments — present content in a flowing, logical, linear layout. Aim to keep content presented in a natural direction – left to right for most languages. Zoom or magnification users will navigate your app from the natural reading side, meaning they may miss any content presented from the right. Consider this if you are presenting a status icon next to text. If your icon is to the right of your text, a magnification user may never realize this status indicator is present.

Keep related controls linked together using semantic view techniques we discussed in Chapter 4 for Android and Chapter 6 for iOS. Linking elements will help to increase the context of your control while making navigation more straightforward.

Race and Nationality

Race is a perfect example of why it's essential to involve people with a range of backgrounds throughout our development process. Ensure that your team includes talented engineers from different countries and cultures. This way, you'll learn much more about your unconscious the assumptions around the people who use your app.

Machine Learning

Machine learning, unfortunately, provides us with some stark examples of where a lack of diverse thinking can backfire. Machine learning is another technology that would fit into any category we discuss in this chapter. But race has explicitly been an area machine learning has proved to be troublesome.

In 2017 AI-powered selfie app, FaceApp stumbled into several controversies as a result of using unchecked stereotypes. One filter they provided changed your face to appear as a different race.[40] While most of us would probably question if this form of digital blackface was a good idea, FaceApp didn't until after their users told them.

In an earlier incident, FaceApp pulled a filter intended to make its users appear more attractive. The so-called hotness filter was a machine learning model that applied transformations to your face. The model based these transformations on what it had learned about people it had been told were "hot." This resulted in the model lightening people's skin tones. FaceApp CEO Yaroslav Goncharov told TechCrunch:

> *It is an unfortunate side-effect of the underlying neural network caused by the training set bias, not intended behavior.*
>
> —FaceApp CEO Yaroslav Goncharov, TechCrunch[41]

Machine learning models are indeed a cause for concern. But the models are not to blame. Machine learning is, despite any hype, like any other computer system – a product of our input. As a result, a significant function of a machine learning model is to reveal our biases. In the case of FaceApp, the group who trained the model had picked beauty based on a European ideal.

While the FaceApp example caused distress and offence, some examples go further. Machine learning systems in use by US courts routinely recommend longer sentences for black offenders compared to

---

[40]Hern, Alex. "FaceApp forced to pull 'racist' filters that allow 'digital blackface'". The Guardian, August 10, 2017. www.theguardian.com/technology/2017/aug/10/faceapp-forced-to-pull-racist-filters-digital-blackface

[41]Lomas, Natasha. "FaceApp apologizes for building a racist AI" Tech Crunch, April 25, 2017. https://techcrunch.com/2017/04/25/faceapp-apologises-for-building-a-racist-ai/

white.[42] The black-box nature of machine learning models compounds this problem. It's not truly possible to test or audit why a model has come to the decision it has.

It's also the case that machine learning is an incredible technology that has helped to power many of the most exciting new features in mobile apps. Image processing filters like we've seen in FaceApp, Snapchat, and Instagram would not be possible without it, neither would the natural language processing that makes accessibility features like Voice Control and Voice Access possible. If you do choose to use machine learning models in your app, consider carefully the application. Have confidence in your data, and try to understand your data's biases before starting. Test, as much as this is possible, to discover where your model is detecting your implicit, unconscious biases. Your model may even help you to improve your data collection.

Localization

Localization is a vast topic. We covered the basics of localizing an app for languages in earlier chapters. But localization is a topic that could comfortably fill a new book. As well as translating your text, remember right-to-left languages require you to consider your app's layout, both in UX design and how you then build the design in your app. Using flowing layouts accommodating varying element sizes will help. Remember, formats are different across locales. Living in the United Kingdom, I am regularly confused when booking trips to the United States and have to double-check I have entered the correct month and day order for dates. If booking apps detected my locale, this would reduce the stress of my booking experience.

---

[42]Liptak, Adam. "Sent to Prison by a Software Program's Secret Algorithms". The New York Times. May 1, 2017. www.nytimes.com/2017/05/01/us/politics/sent-to-prison-by-a-software-programs-secret-algorithms.html

Even if your app is only available in a single market, we live in a global society. In 2017 the US Census Bureau found that nearly 22% of Americans spoke a language other than English when at home.[43] That's around 70 million people in the United States who would likely find your app less complicated to use if another language was available to them.

Developing Accessibility and Inclusion

I'm genuinely grateful you've chosen to pick up my book, not just because this book means a lot to me personally but because I'm always excited when people want to know more about mobile accessibility and inclusion. We have a privileged position as people who are shaping how the modern world works and progresses. And we have opportunities that colleagues in other fields don't. If a building with step-only access finds people can't access it, replacing the steps is a big job. In software, we can identify and fix similar issues rapidly. Then we can have the improved software in the hands of our customers within the time it takes for an app review.

Hopefully, with this new knowledge, you'll begin to identify potential accessibility issues in your app. As you gain more knowledge, please pass this on as you gain confidence. Arrange workshops, or speak at a lunch-and-learn session. For larger teams, consider starting an accessibility community of practice program. Sharing potential issues and fixes will only result in a better outcome for your customer.

From my experience, most of our fellow developers are interested in accessibility and want to do the right thing. They're sometimes just lacking the knowledge about how to do this.

---

[43]"New American Community Survey Statistics for Income, Poverty and Health Insurance Available for States and Local Areas", United States Census Bureau. September 14, 2017. `www.census.gov/newsroom/press-releases/2017/acs-single-year.html`

A11y Community

Much like the iOS and Android communities as a whole, there's a vibrant and dedicated digital accessibility community. This community generally uses the acronym A11y. We take the A and Y from accessibility, and the 11 refers to the 11 letters in between. It also creates a pleasing homonym for ally. Usefully this acronym also helps to differentiate people who are passionate about making accessible technology from those who use accessibility features. If you're looking to find out more about the accessible technology community, try searching Twitter or LinkedIn for #A11y. I run a Twitter account, @MobileA11y, to share mobile-related accessibility content.

Meetups and Conferences

The A11y community hosts a range of conferences and meetups discussing best practices and advancements. These are great places to expand your knowledge and meet experts to ask for more information when you've met a particularly sticky accessibility bug. I also got the opportunity to learn British Sign Language at one event.

There are many accessibility meetups and conferences throughout the world, but I've attended, and can highly recommend, both Accessibility London[44] and Accessibility Nottingham[45] in the United Kingdom. While I've not had the opportunity to attend, mobile accessibility specialist Paul J. Adam is an organizer of Austin Accessibility and Inclusive Design meetup[46] in Austin, Texas. And mobile accessibility expert Jon Gibbins

---

[44]www.meetup.com/London-Accessibility-Meetup/

[45]www.accessibilitynottingham.co.uk

[46]www.meetup.com/a11yATX/

is an organizer of Bristol Inclusive Design and Development meetup[47] in Bristol, United Kingdom.

Accessibility Scotland[48] in Edinburgh, United Kingdom, is a 1-day accessibility conference with some incredibly thought-provoking talks. You can find videos, transcripts, and slides for these talks on their blog.[49]

---

[47]www.meetup.com/Bristol-Inclusive-Design-and-Development/
[48]https://accessibility.scot
[49]https://accessibility.scot/blog/

Index

A

© Rob Whitaker 2020
R. Whitaker, *Developing Inclusive Mobile Apps*,
https://doi.org/10.1007/978-1-4842-5814-9

Printed in the United States
By Bookmasters